Praise for Mad About Us
by Gary and Carrie Oliver

"Dr. Gary Oliver is not only my key mentor in life, but the person who actually helped me really understand what's beneath the power of anger and what you can do about it."

—**Gary Smalley,** author of *The DNA of Relationships*

"Anger has been a destroyer of many marriages, but one of the powerful things Gary and Carrie show us is how to harness the energy of anger to lead us into a deeper level of intimacy in marriage. Not only is this a clear, practical book on enriching our marriages, it is also an intimate and honest look into the marriage of the authors. I've known Gary and Carrie for years, and they lived the reality of what they've written."

—**David Stoop,** PhD, author of *Better Than Ever: Seven*

"E ... it is inevitable
and G ... v to use your
conflic ... ed to cultivate
deeper ... t, but because
of it! \ ... for your rela-
tionshi ... *ad About Us.*"

Time-Starved

Marriage

"If you're serious about having a passionate, caring, connected marriage . . . then walk to the counter and buy this book right now. We cannot think of a more courageous couple than Gary and Carrie Oliver. What they learned in the battles they faced over the years can help keep your marriage from becoming a war zone. Even more, their 'I can do that!' wisdom can turn 'mad' into 'madly in love' with your spouse."

—**John and Cindy Trent,** The Center for StrongFamilies

"If you want to take your marriage from good to great, if you want to discover the DNA of intimacy in ways that can transform your marriage, then you must read *Mad About Us*. You'll be pleasantly surprised at how easy it can be to increase the passion and deepen the intimacy in your marriage. This is a book you'll read more than once and recommend to your friends."

> —**Tim Clinton,** President, American Association of Christian Counselors.

"Years ago we planted two trees . . . feet from each other and watched them grow over the years. In the early stages they were both nourished by the sun and rain and grew independent of each other. Then their root systems went deeper and began to intertwine with each other to the point where today if you look deep beneath the surface they appear as one. But it didn't happen without struggle, roots wrapping around each other, at times crowding each other out and fighting for nourishment. And today they bring shade, strength, and beautiful color to our lives. A bit like becoming one in marriage. We bring our own root systems into our union, as we grow we fight for our place and ultimately become so interdependent and connected that we can't discern where one of us begins and the other ends. Our dear friends, Gary and Carrie Oliver, bring a vulnerable, inside look at God's grace in taking two strong trees and making them one, not in spite of the struggles but because they walked through the storms of life . . . together. The Olivers unpack an inside look into the God-given emotion of anger and how they not only grew through the struggles but glorified God and experienced the intimacy that can only come through the struggles. Gary and Carrie are two of our heroes. Read this book, *Mad About Us*, and they will become your heroes as well."

> —**Dr. Gary and Barb Rosberg,** authors of *Divorce-Proof Your Marriage*

GARY J. OLIVER
PhD

CARRIE OLIVER
MA

MAD
ABOUT
US

MOVING FROM
ANGER TO
INTIMACY
WITH YOUR SPOUSE

BETHANYHOUSE
PUBLISHERS

Published by Bethany House Publishers
11400 Hampshire Avenue South
Bloomington, Minnesota 55438

Bethany House Publishers is a division of
Baker Publishing Group, Grand Rapids, Michigan.

Printed in the United States of America

Library of Congress Cataloging-in-Publication Data

Oliver, Gary J.
    Mad about us : moving from anger to intimacy with your spouse / Gary J. Oliver, Carrie Oliver.
        p. cm.
    Summary: "Gives couples practical, biblical ways to transform the energy of unhealthy anger into a healthy passion that can free them to deal with core fears, hurts, and frustrations in ways that build trust and lead to deeper intimacy"—Provided by publisher.
    ISBN-13: 978-0-7642-0449-4 (pbk. : alk. paper)
    ISBN-10: 0-7642-0449-1 (pbk. : alk. paper)
    1. Marriage—Religious aspects—Christianity. 2. Anger—Religious aspects—Christianity. I. Oliver, Carrie, 1959–2007. II. Title.
    BV835.O45   2007
    248.8'44—dc22   2007023973

In celebration of the vibrant life of

Carrie E. Oliver

<small>APRIL 21, 1959–JULY 2, 2007</small>

Loving wife
Beloved mother
Caring daughter and sister
Loyal friend
Wise counselor
A lover of Jesus

"Jesus said to her, 'I am the resurrection and the life.
He who believes in me will live, even though he dies;
and whoever lives and believes in me will never die.'"
—John 11:25–26

For the last two years of her life, my wife, Carrie, courageously battled metastatic pancreatic cancer. She had been given a three to six month prognosis, but with great faith in the goodness, grace, and sovereignty of her Lord Jesus Christ, with amazing courage and determination, and with the prayer support of friends, Carrie lived for two more years. Those two years were gifts to me, our family, our friends, and thousands of people who knew Carrie only from the "Journal of Hope" she kept on her Web site (*www.carrieshealth.com*). Shortly after we finished writing *Mad About Us,* Carrie went from the arms of her family to the arms of the Lord she loved and had so faithfully served.

The first book we wrote together was *Raising Sons and Loving It!* and it contained some of the very practical things we learned from raising our three sons and helping many other parents raise theirs. This book, *Mad About Us,* was a special joy and truly a labor of love. It was inspired by our love for each other and our love for what we knew marriage could become—a miracle we had witnessed firsthand.

It was such a privilege for us to write it together. Carrie poured a lot of her heart into this book. She believed the message because we had experienced it, we saw literally hundreds of couples use it in our counseling work, and we shared it with thousands of other couples in our marriage enrichment conferences—all with great results.

There were times she wasn't feeling well, especially after some of her chemotherapy treatments, when I would find her at the computer writing her heart out. I would encourage her to just rest and take it easy, but she would always say that it was good medicine for her, and the idea of couples being helped to discover a new way to build greater intimacy actually gave her energy and thrilled her—as it does me.

While Carrie is no longer with us, I am still madly in love with her and even more deeply committed to sharing the message of how to experience and enjoy an intimate, passionate, growth-focused, and Christ-centered marriage. Carrie's greatest desire was that God would be glorified and that people would see the difference He made in her life and in our marriage and our family. I pray that God will use this book to accomplish that in your life and in your marriage.

—Gary Oliver

CONTENTS

Introduction | 11

1. And They Lived Happily Ever After | 15

2. Designed to Experience Intimacy | 25

3. Barriers to Intimacy | 35

4. The Emotional Side of Intimacy | 47

5. From Intimacy to Anger | 61

6. The Myths of Anger | 77

7. The Many Faces of Anger | 95

8. Making Anger Work for You | 111

9. Intimate Conflict: A Pathway to Intimacy | 131

10. Seven Simple Steps Through Conflict to Intimacy | 153

11. Forgiveness: The Healing Oil of Intimacy | 171

12. Diving Deep Into an Intimate Marriage | 183

Epilogue | 193

Discussion Guide | 201

Endnotes | 219

Acknowledgments | 221

INTRODUCTION

When I pick up a book I wonder, *What qualifies this author to write on this subject? Does he or she have some understanding as to the plight of my life? Will this book be relevant to me?* You might be asking similar questions about *Mad About Us,* yet another book on marriage. Who are these people, where did they come from, and what do they have to offer me?

WHO WE ARE

As we write this book Gary and I have been married for twenty-six years, raised three sons, changed jobs and moved four times, acquired several degrees and a daughter-in-law along the way, walked through cancer, and lost one of our sons. Over the past thirty years Gary has conducted over one hundred weddings, and we've provided premarital counseling for more than one thousand couples and marriage counseling for well over five thousand couples. We have taught marriage seminars and healthy relationship classes and written articles for various magazines. We have studied communication, conflict resolution, the differences between men and women, emotions and godly ways to express them.

We come to you with this book straight from our hearts and experience. You see, we are a real couple that, like you, has conflicts and differences that continue to catch us by surprise! Both Gary and I are still amazed and puzzled by the way we think, act, feel or don't feel, communicate, and generally do life very differently from each other. Sometimes we like the differences and sometimes we get mad—frustrated, lonely, hurt, distant—when differences and conflict surface.

WHY WE WROTE THE BOOK

Aside from our differences and ongoing frustrations, we have grown an intimate marriage and believe you can do the same. We cannot imagine life without each other. Sometimes we can imagine a day without the other, but life—no way! We want that for your marriage too.

Without exception every couple we have worked with began their marriage with a proclamation of their love and a commitment to stay together until "death do us part." That's how we started ours. We all talked about our dreams for a lifetime of love, trust, safety, security, and deep levels of intimacy.

In many cases the couples we have worked with talked about being madly in love or mad about each other. Unfortunately the reality is that once a couple gets married the "mad" that was a synonym for passionate love often becomes a synonym for unhealthy frustration. That frustration can easily turn to an unhealthy anger that discourages hearts, divides couples, and often destroys relationships.

The tragedy is that it doesn't take long for the "mad about each other" to turn into mad *at* each other and for the relationship to go into a downhill slide. There are a gazillion reasons why some marriages fall apart while others survive but are characterized by mediocrity. However, the vast majority of those failed or mediocre marriages have at their core the inability to understand differences, deal with the emotion of anger in healthy ways, and engage in healthy and constructive conflict.

WHAT'S IN THE BOOK FOR YOU

This is a book about intimacy. It's a book about restoring the positive passion that we all had at the beginning of our marriage journey. Our hope is that this book will help you to enjoy a long-lasting and mutually satisfying marriage relationship characterized by intimacy. Our goal is that after reading this book you will better understand how dealing with anger and conflict can lead you to that intimacy. Over the years the many couples we've worked with have taught us that if we don't understand how to deal with unhealthy anger and engage in constructive conflict, we will never experience the deep levels of intimacy that led us into marriage in the first place.

Mad About Us seeks to offer hope. If we had to put into one word what has brought us through a marriage that has lasted twenty-six years it is *hope*. We have never lost hope for a better tomorrow and a better marriage. The hope comes from a belief system that says God can change my heart and my perspective and I can learn new ways of understanding God's Word, myself, and my spouse. The good news is that we can always learn something new, or even better, recommit to that which we already know.

We have never lost hope, even as we've both walked through cancer, and even after we lost our son Matt. We have both had tremendous pain, confronted fear, and wondered about tomorrow, but we have never given up hope. I received an article on hope early on in my diagnosis, and I have clung to the words of that article. Hope is what sustains us to live on this earth whether we are struggling through difficulty or things are going well. I have come to love my God deeply as He has walked this road of cancer and grief with me. Writing this book is a blessing and privilege for me and one that I treasure as I share with you the hope God has for you in any area of struggle in your life, even in your marriage. Won't you cling to hope as well?

Reading this book you will contemplate what God had in mind when He created us in His image. He designed us to experience intimacy. Have you been afraid of anger? Are you easily frustrated? Do emotions seem to be a foreign concept? Or are you a person who can't seem to round up all the emotions you feel, overwhelming yourself and those around you? Does the word *conflict* make you run in the opposite direction? You can learn new ways of understanding anger and expressing emotions that can be helpful both to your spouse and to you.

Would you like a deeper experience of intimacy in your marriage?

We would like to show you how to move through conflict and anger to that intimacy, a safe place to be both real and vulnerable, a place to discover more about yourself and your spouse.

We pray that from a renewed hope you will be changed and that your intimacy with your spouse will be greater and deeper than you have ever experienced. As you begin to read this book, and better yet apply what you read, our hope is that you will be inspired, challenged, and even changed with time.

—Carrie Oliver

AND THEY LIVED HAPPILY EVER AFTER

On a beautiful December day in Nebraska, in a gorgeous church setting, Gary and I stood before a crowd of people and said our marriage vows to one another. Lovely things like, "I will love you unconditionally. I will honor and respect you and be with you in sickness and in health." We had beautiful praise and worship music, took Communion, and lit our unity candle, symbolizing becoming one. It was a magical, dreamy, one-in-a-million day. I don't think Ken and Barbie could have done it better!

Like many couples, by the second day of marriage we began to discover that we were very different from each other. During our engagement we saw each other only on the weekends, giving a glimpse of the best of who we were. On the second day of our marriage we began to feel emotions that we had not felt yet with each other. I noticed that Gary could get distracted, it seemed, very easily. I felt rejected because he was not paying attention like I thought he did when we were dating and engaged. He noticed that I had more opinions than before, and the opinions seemed to be the opposite of his own, leaving him feeling disrespected and unheard. The result? We felt insecure and misunderstood. The "mad about each other" became just "mad."

We have dreams when we commit to marriage. We have expectations that we have found our soul mate, our prince or princess. We dream of making a safe haven where we can be vulnerable, accepted, understood, and loved. We desire friendship, companionship, and sometimes partnership. But real-life marriage doesn't always measure up to our dreams, and we often become disappointed and angry.

GOD'S DESIGN

Miraculously, God created man and woman in His image (Genesis 1:27). Isn't this wonderful to contemplate, that each and every one of us is walking around with the image of God? Oh to grasp this truth and live it out rather than live as the fallen, sinful beings we became when wrong choices were made.

God had something good in mind when He brought man and woman together. He said that it was not a good thing for the man to be alone. He brought forth the woman from the man and gave them to each other (Genesis 2:18–22). Marriage is a place where we have the opportunity to feel close to someone else, so close that loneliness does not overwhelm us. God created the sexual experience for a man and woman in marriage to enjoy with delight and freedom. Pure pleasure. Another place to feel safe, vulnerable, and not alone.

God also designed the marriage relationship to reflect who He is. Because we are made in His image, because we are in relationship, we now can show the world what intimate relationship looks like. Marriage is both a reflection and a microcosm of a personal relationship with God. Marriage is a place to become more holy and to demonstrate holiness to a fallen world.

God's design for marriage is that we would experience intimacy with Him and then with each other. Do not be discouraged if you are reading along and find that this does not ring true in your marriage!

Remember that thing called hope? If everyone had cooperated in the garden of Eden and followed God's rules, there would be no need for any marriage book on the market! But we all know that is not what happened. Sin entered the world and sin entered marriage. When this took place, the man and woman began to hide from each other. They hid their bodies, their hearts, and their minds. If they did it right there with God so close to them, even to His calling out in an audible voice, "Where are you?" (Genesis 3:9), then it is not surprising that we do the same in our world today, not exactly the garden of Eden.

EVER AFTER, BUT NOT ALWAYS HAPPILY!

In our fallen world, we continue to experience the effects of what took place that day sin entered into the picture. We began to hide from God and from one another. Intimacy was invaded, and we were left with two ways of coping. We have found as we work with couples, and in our own marriage, that these two ways are hiding and blaming. Pretty close to what Adam and Eve experienced that day! They hid from God, and lots of blaming took place. "She did it, God, and you were the one who gave her to me," Adam proclaimed (see Genesis 3:12). The snake got a bad rap, and everyone started hiding themselves with those fig leaves.

A couple sat across from me in a recent session and I listened to the same story that I hear over and over again. Jason resists coming home at night because he feels Melissa does not meet his needs and blames him for much of her emotional turmoil. She says that he doesn't pay enough attention to her, all he cares about is himself, and he only plays with the baby because he is supposed to. Meanwhile he feels that she is only in touch with her own feelings, completely misunderstands him, and does not encourage him as a husband, father, and provider. They argue, then retreat. Nothing is resolved and intimacy is hindered. The "happily ever after" us becomes the "mad at each other" us.

Oddly, this same scenario has been going on for centuries, and we are not doing anything much differently to change it. We continue to deal with conflict and differences in the same ways that Adam and Eve did back in the garden.

Blaming is a very large part of how we function as human beings in most of our relationships. (If you are parents, you see it happen all the time with the kids. One sibling is constantly pointing the finger at the other sibling.) We simply do not want to take responsibility for our behavior, and it rarely occurs to us to sit back and try to understand the heart of our spouse. We are not intentional about how we listen to them even in their emotional experience of hurt or anger or fear. If we are completely honest, once we start to feel the emotions, we begin to focus on our need at the moment and how our spouse should be meeting it or at least listening to us.

We can become good at hiding when we find that blaming doesn't get the results we wanted, so now we just don't share at all. Trouble is, we are still experiencing emotions at some level and we sacrifice intimacy with our spouse when we hide our heart from their heart.

But "happily" is still God's plan for us! He desires for us to experience love, friendship, and deep intimacy, but we must come to grips with what is going on in the ever after that is not so happy, and the sooner the better. If we don't, we become disillusioned and defeated and feel as if our expectations were all for naught! This can set us up for a lifetime of marital defeat rather than marital bliss.

DIFFERENTLY EVER AFTER

What is it that we just don't get? God created us male and female from the beginning. Our differences are part of His design. But it seems when sin entered the world, the differences that were once helpful to intimacy became hindrances to intimacy. We can see that our body structures are very different on the outside. That is a good thing!

What we react to are the major differences on the inside. We may even blame each other for being different.

The female brain is constructed very differently than the male brain. Females live in the relational and emotional hemispheres of the brain fairly consistently.[1] This is due to more connectors between the right and left hemispheres. A female secretes higher levels of oxytocin, sometimes called the "bonding" chemical.[2] This chemical is secreted at greater levels during childbirth to aid in the bonding process between the mother and the child. Females reach out to bond in their relationships due to higher oxytocin levels.

Men, on the other hand, secrete very little of this chemical; it is most likely to be at higher levels right after having sexual intercourse. While testosterone drives the male in their sexual desire, they do feel very bonded after sex due to the rise in the oxytocin level. A woman wants to bond before sexual intercourse, while a man feels bonding afterward. We would become less mad about this whole sexual dilemma if we just understood these simple differences as male and female and sought to meet each other's needs. Husbands, bond a little with your wife, and wives, have sex with your husband, and you will both get an oxytocin high! We know it is not that simple—we live in the real world like you do. But if we recognize and appreciate our differences, we can avoid doing the same thing that does not work over and over again.

Entire books have been dedicated to teaching on the male and female brain and chemical differences. Our "happily ever after" is affected when we don't understand that men are more compartmentalized in their approach to life and relationships and emotions, while most women are constantly working out of a relational- and emotional-thinking process. This is why men do not remember emotional experiences as well as women do. They may remember facts about sports events or what is happening on Wall Street, but what our tears were about two weeks ago may elude them.

A woman's brain has been shown not to rest at all, while a man's brain will need mental naps. Beware, ladies, to watch for the stare on his face. He may be taking a mental nap, giving you the signal that a deep emotional connection and conversation is not going to happen! If you don't want to get mad and frustrated or hurt, then wait until that brain of his is awake and alert and trying to make the switch to the relational compartment.

Testosterone is a major player in the male. A man has thirty times more testosterone than a woman has. Testosterone drives the sexual desire and may increase competitiveness and aggression. As we mentioned, women secrete oxytocin, which drives them to bond. In conflict a woman may try to bond with her husband. She does this by trying to talk, relate, get her emotions out, and often because she does not understand the differences, she may expect him to function in similar ways. He has to actively work at going to the compartment in his brain that is relational, emotional. He often does not understand this about himself and perceives her advances as pressure to perform. Often this scenario results in misunderstanding, sometimes leading to anger and frustration.

PERSONALITY DIFFERENCES

There are gender differences, but we are also different in the ways we see or approach our world because of our personalities. We know we have different personalities; we may even say, "My spouse has a lot of personality!" What we liked about our spouse and his or her personality can become a frustration after the marriage vows when we try to make everyday life work.

I like details and the experience of the here and now, while Gary likes vision and dreams and planning for the future. I remember in the first year of our marriage Gary started talking about taking a trip to Europe. We had absolutely no money. I had been on a plane only one time, and that was to California for our honeymoon. Now he was talking about flying to England, spending two weeks there and then another two weeks on the continent of Europe, for a total of a month. I felt fear from the tip of my head to the bottom of my toes. Where were we going to get the money? Would we have jobs when we got back? How would we drive around? And where would we stay? Who is this man? I did not join him in this crazy dream. Every detail of why we could not possibly do this came to my mind and out of my mouth.

We experienced several of these scenarios in our first year of marriage. It was a blessing to us that Gary was in his doctoral program. During his program he became familiar with different personality types in a personality assessment class. This helped us tremendously as we discovered that neither of us was out to destroy the other's dreams or security or privacy. We came to our world with different personalities, and what we needed to do was understand this about each other, affirm our differences, and work through them.

It is so easy to get mad when we don't see eye to eye. Personality is a huge area of difference that most couples simply do not understand. When our spouse reacts and thinks differently than we do, we may take it personally. I was very guilty of doing this early on in our marriage. I am a feeling person, which means I make decisions based on my feelings. When Gary did not always feel the same as I did, or even worse, had some rational, logical solution to offer, I felt misunderstood. I felt as if my feelings were not being heard. He felt very similar when I did not listen to and utilize his well-thought-out, very rational solutions to my problems or our problems. We ended up blaming each other for not understanding and learned fast what not to talk about, eventually hiding from the issues. (Not happily ever after.)

JESUS BRINGS THE HAPPY INTO THE EVER AFTER

After about fifteen years of marriage (hopefully you will get this faster than we did), we began to really see what Jesus could do in this marriage of ours. You see, having tools and skills, listening and communicating, resolving conflict, and expressing emotions are all very helpful when trying to grow a marriage. But even when we try to implement these skills, we must remember what God had in mind when He created marriage. Most Christians would say that Christ makes a difference in their marriage, but most do not function in this manner. We don't wake up in the morning saying to ourselves, "Today I will be Christ to my spouse." But we are very aware of how our spouse is *not* being Christ to us.

We suggest starting each day with a prayer that goes something like this: *Jesus, look at me. Show me my weaknesses and strengths. How am I doing loving my partner? Jesus, if I were kinder and gentler, what would that look like? I think I might speak more softly. I would listen to my spouse today. I would say "I love you," and I would touch this person you gave me. I would say I was sorry. Because you love me, Jesus, I might even be willing to face conflict with my spouse or take responsibility for something I said or did. I might let my spouse see my heart as I am doing with you now. Thank you for this mate you have given me. Help me to see what I need to change in order to love well. I know that you love me well in spite of myself. I believe that as I do these things and as I pray this prayer consistently I can work through my emotions better. I can look at not only how I feel but at how we both feel in our marriage, and that gives me hope for a deeper intimacy.*

What God desires for us is that we be transformed in the marriage relationship—that we, with each day, would look just a little bit more like Him because we spent the day with our spouse. Wow! I know for us many days did not exactly end with this type of result. The exciting news is that when we are functioning out of what God planned for us, we experience deeper and deeper levels of intimacy both with Him and each other. This is a great motivator to change and do things differently, especially when we grasp what intimacy is. Genuine intimacy goes beyond the soul mate idea. Our culture, Christian culture included, promotes the idea that we "find" our soul mate, when in fact what God had in mind is that we "become" a soul mate.

Do you want that in your marriage? Do you want to know more about God's idea of intimacy and what it means to be transformed and have a transformed relationship? That is our heart for you and your marriage. In the next chapter we'll see that God created us for intimacy, and we'll look at the components of intimacy.

You may think that "happily ever after" can't happen or that "content ever after" is the best you can hope for, but we know that God wants great joy for us in marriage, more than mere contentment. He desires for us to be vibrant, Jesus-emulating human beings in love with each other. He wants us to demonstrate to the world that marriage works, and it works because Jesus died on a cross for us so that we might have life, and life more abundantly! Jesus does bring the happy into the "ever after."

SMALL BEGINNINGS

1. Identify the disappointments of the "ever after" in your marriage. What were your expectations when you got married?
2. What are some differences that seem to plague your relationship? Are there differences that you enjoy?
3. What are some of the issues in your marriage that you hide from or have decided not to address?
4. Do you tend to blame your spouse for the problems in your marriage?
5. How much is Jesus allowed into your relationship? How can you begin to change the level at which He makes a difference?
6. How can you become a better soul mate?

CHAPTER

2

DESIGNED TO EXPERIENCE INTIMACY

One reason many of us married our spouse is that they seemed to know us better than anyone else we'd ever dated. They listened to us, paid attention to our interests and needs, and really seemed to care about even the little things in our lives. We assumed that this would be just the beginning of an amazing, deep, passionate, trusting, and intimate marriage. When we get married we pack expectations right inside the luggage (or baggage, as some would call it) that we take with us on the honeymoon and into the marriage.

INSTANT SOUL MATES?

The media leads us to believe that intimacy is easy to create, perhaps even on a first date! Instant soul mates! We may question our ability to experience intimacy with our spouse when we don't feel the soul mate thing. Because we see instant intimacy everywhere we turn, we come to expect that we will feel it easily as well and become confused or frustrated when we don't.

During the months of our engagement Gary and I talked and dreamed and shared our hearts. We prayed together, we shared our ideas on books we read, we even had fun planning the wedding with little conflict! We felt so close. We thought we were very intimate. Shortly after the wedding it was as if I woke up next to someone I did not know. Our differences started coming at us fast, and instead of working through them or appreciating them, we bumped up against them hard. We felt unheard and we felt unknown.

We hear from many couples in our enrichment seminars and in our counseling that they had similar experiences. We have a lifetime of marriage to get to know each other, but we don't think it will take that long! One day it hits us that the person who seemed to be a soul mate has suddenly turned into an adversary.

In the counseling office, I (Carrie) find that people sometimes limit their interpretation of intimacy to the bedroom. True, this is a great place to experience some of what intimacy has to offer, but the bedroom is not the place where intimacy begins or ends. In fact, if there isn't intimacy outside of the bedroom, there will never be the deepest or most fulfilling levels of intimacy inside of the bedroom.

Intimacy can be extremely energizing, as well as completely draining. Think of it; we want to know and be known. God created us for intimacy, and so we long for it, but we often experience emotional conflict trying to gain it. As a result of our disappointment, discouragement, and frustration, we often experience anger. Anger in marriage can tend to dry up the intimacy from the relationship, and we are left thirsting for something more.

INTIMACY: WHAT IS IT?

What did God have in mind for this whole idea of growing intimacy with our life-spouse? We were built with a need for connection, to bond, to belong. It is something God instilled in us when He created us. We have within us a need for another to know us and a need to experience safety in our strengths and in our weaknesses. We have been created to have this closeness with Jesus Christ, and we have been created to seek this out with other humans. As we talk of intimacy in this chapter we will be addressing intimacy within the boundaries of marriage. This is the deepest form of intimacy that a human being has the potential to experience while here on earth because it encompasses the heart, the soul, the intellect, the emotions, and unlike other intimate relationships, the physical-sexual part.

Merriam-Webster's New Collegiate Dictionary defines *intimate* as, "belonging to or characterizing one's deepest nature, marked by very close association, contact or familiarity, of a very personal or private nature." Intimacy is an aspect of marriage that evolves over time. We must view intimacy as something we work toward as an artist paints with painstaking strokes of the brush to create a beautiful piece of art. Most of us do not understand this developmental process, and we get frustrated with how tedious it can be to go the distance to become intimate.

Intimacy is good for marriage! Like a beautiful flower garden, intimacy is something that has to be cultivated, attended to, watered, and cared for. Without proper care it will be stunted, the color will be dull, the bud may never open or never start to grow, or it will die prematurely.

When I think of intimacy that develops over time I think of Dwight and Julie. They went into their marriage relationship understanding that marriage takes effort and that intimacy is not instant. They grew their marriage by daily watering their relationship with love, affection, and romance. They understood that they both needed Christ. Dwight and Julie took time for dates and tune-ups, getting away to talk about how they were doing. When they did feel hurt they did not let hurt build up. Built-up hurt and anger are like weeds choking out the intimacy from a relationship. They wrap themselves around what is healthy and simply kill it off. When we focus on hurt and anger that soon becomes all we see.

Dwight and Julie were able to put their pride aside and seek help when they felt they could not deal with problems on their own. They watered, fertilized, and cultivated their marriage with prayer, vulnerability, and trust, assuming the best in each other. This couple could then turn around and provide great insight as mentors for newly married couples. They had grown their intimacy rather than let it be stunted or choked out by not giving intimacy the attention it so needs.

There are different expressions of intimacy. Sometimes we just need our spouse to know what we are thinking. Walking through cancer as Gary and I each have, we get scared at times and we need to share those scary thoughts. Gary loves to dream, and even though I prefer the present day of my life, he feels very close to me when he can talk about what he dreams for the future. I don't have to have the same dream; I only need to listen to his and encourage him.

Intimacy often requires that we do activities together. There are many types of recreational activities to share, but one dear couple in our community group is sharing time together right now that is a big sacrifice on the husband's part. His wife has class many nights out of the week after they work all day. She is finishing her master's degree. He joins her for the one-hour drive from their home to her class. While this might not be his favorite recreational activity, they are together and their intimacy is building. We delight as a group to watch their intimacy grow!

Intimacy is expressed in how we share our emotions. I let Gary know me better when I name my feelings and tell him about them, and I know him better when he can do some of the same. Some couples can really get stuck here if they are unaware of their emotions, and that is why we devote so much of this book to understanding emotions and how to express them.

The experience of sharing the sexual relationship is truly God's great gift in marriage. It is not the only expression of intimacy, but it is an ingredient to creating intimacy, and it requires intimacy to experience it to its fullest capacity.

In addition, things like acceptance, affection, vulnerability, safety, communication, nurturing, kindness, empathy, listening, quality time, dating, romance, etc., all contribute to intimacy. But there are a few other key components to intimacy within a relationship. What are the brushstrokes that create on this canvas of marriage a beautiful piece of art called intimacy? As we explore the components of intimacy, keep in mind that they are all found in Scripture. Remember, intimacy was God's idea; He is the one who created it.

SENSE OF SELF

Intimacy begins with understanding that we are designed in God's image, and to be intimate with another person we must bring to the relationship a healthy and godly sense of *self*. As I know who God created me to be and I embrace these parts I can then bring them to Gary and embrace who God created him to be. I know my strengths and my weaknesses. When I can admit my weaknesses and I don't feel I have to defend my strengths, I am more likely to be safe to embrace his strengths and weaknesses. He then is free to be who God created him to be. Bringing my self to him in intimacy can help me to see more of who God created me to be and more of who God created him to be, releasing us both to bring great glory to His kingdom.

Understanding and embracing self can be a looming task, and it too is a developmental process. Often we bring a damaged self or a misunderstood self to the marriage relationship. Many people I work with are looking for their spouse to complete them. When their spouse does not seem to be able to perform this task, anger, hurt, and frustration are often felt, and the result is broken trust. But our spouse cannot fix us, and in fact many of us do not want to be fixed by our spouse. And although our spouse cannot fix us, marriage needs to be a safe place to bring our hurts, our losses, our grief, and our weaknesses. I cannot know all of Gary's hurts to the extent that I understand them completely, but I can listen to him; I can affirm him and encourage him.

Tina had experienced sexual abuse as a child. Her husband, Kevin, did not show fear of this or anger but simply let Tina know that his heart wanted to walk alongside hers as she learned to trust him and that he would not hurt her. Kevin did not blame any sexual problems they had on Tina. He let her know that he had hurts as well from his childhood and that they could work through their hurts together. Sometimes our pasts are so painful we need to pursue counseling. Our partner can offer to be a part of that process if it will be helpful.

Our spouse is a part of our lives to complete the parts of who we are in a partnership of mutual love. If I am looking for Gary to fix these damaged parts of me, then he will fail. But if I trust him to allow me to talk about these parts and to walk with me on my journey with Christ healing me, then I bring a self that is healthy and seeking to let him know me. And I can enjoy knowing these parts of him as well. Then I am also willing to walk with him on his journey of healing. There is only one healer, our God in heaven. We are here to be reflections of His love, sometimes getting it right and sometimes getting it wrong, but working at bringing ourselves to our spouse and working at knowing who our spouse is in healthy and helpful ways.

TRUST

Another component of intimacy, and a very important one, is the ability to *trust and be trusted*. This is tricky for most of us. Isaiah 12:2 says, "See, God has come to save me. I will trust in him and not be afraid. The Lord God is my strength and my song; he has given me victory" (NLT). Trust first begins with trusting God that He loves us and that He has provided salvation for us and He is willing to walk with us on this earth in the form of His Son, Jesus Christ. We also need to understand that as a result of sin, none of us can possibly achieve pure trustworthiness while we are on this earth. I find in my own experience of being married to Gary that it is easier for me to expect him to be trustworthy but to give myself some extra leeway, because after all I am not perfect! But I need to give him the same grace.

Many people come from backgrounds where they learned not to

trust. Others have made mistakes over and over again and failed at being trustworthy. When we understand that intimacy demands trust at its core, we understand that we have to change our past experience and become someone who can be trusted. Our behavior needs to communicate to our spouse, "I do not want to hurt you in any way, and even if I do please understand that in the deepest parts of my heart my intention for you is good not bad. I will work to gain your trust again if I fail." Trusting and being trusted is something we build together as we work on intimacy.

Primary to being able to trust and to being trusted is our belief in a God who is trustworthy. If we do not trust the Lord in all of our daily life experiences, how can we really understand the whole concept of trust? Let's explore this "God trust" in Scripture. Following are some of the many verses that talk about God as trustworthy.

> Trust in the Lord with all your heart and lean not on your own understanding. (Proverbs 3:5)
> For you have been my hope, O Sovereign Lord. (Psalm 71:5)
> He trusts in the Lord; let the Lord rescue him. Let him deliver him since he delights in him. (Psalm 22:8)

As Gary and I have walked through our marriage, through parenting, and especially through cancer, we have had to come face to face with the question, can I trust my God? What we have found is that He is a God to be trusted. He has answered prayers, and He does reveal His precious love to us. It may not always look like we want it to look, but the fact remains that He delights in those who delight in Him (Psalm 37). We encourage you to seek Scripture in order to understand further this trustworthy God of ours.

Over the course of a life relationship, trust will probably be broken at some level, requiring the components of *honesty* and *forgiveness* in order to reestablish trust and continue to build and develop deep intimacy.

HONESTY

At the Christian university where Gary and I work, the students are looking for authenticity. Somewhere inside of their hearts they intuit that honesty is a treasure and a lost art. It is, in fact, something that the human heart needs from another human heart. Certainly I cannot be intimate with another unless I am willing to be honest. Honest about how I feel, what I think, what I have done, who I am, what I long for, where I have been. To be intimate with a marriage partner we need this type of honesty. You see, intimacy requires trust and trust requires honesty. When we are willing to be honest we can confess our wrongful behavior and ask for forgiveness, another component of intimacy.

FORGIVENESS

As we have said, anger and frustration seem to be an occupational hazard of marriage. Somewhere in the marriage process we all will experience being angry and frustrated with our beloved. Things like the full trash can that didn't get taken out for the 20 millionth time, the forgotten phone call, the words that were insensitive, the lack of encouragement or touch, or the disrespect. The ability to ask for forgiveness and to forgive takes us to a deeper level of intimacy. Even in the most significant places of betrayal, such as adultery or secret addictions, intimacy can be restored when honesty and forgiveness and repentance take place to repair the relationship.

It is important to understand that forgiveness does not mean instant restoration of the relationship, but it is a step toward restoration. Forgiveness means we eventually let go of anger; we do not allow anger to keep its grip on us. When we forgive we go deeper and away from anger to the places where we hurt or have hurt our spouse. We get behind the eyes and experience of our spouse and see their world from their perspective. That is called empathy. We so want our partner to empathize with us, to get inside our heart. Can we do that for them, even when we are so angry we want to lash out or hide? Anger gives us the opportunity to look at what we are really feeling, whether we are hurt or afraid. As we do this we can also look at our spouse beyond their anger to the underlying hurt or fear and reach inside their heart to touch them as we ask for forgiveness or we offer the gift of forgiveness. Oh how vital, how intimate!

BOUNDARIES

One final component central to laying the foundation for intimacy is the ability to form healthy and godly *boundaries*. Boundaries is one of those buzz words in our culture. But what are boundaries and why are they foundational for intimacy? We can only understand boundaries if we understand who we are in Christ. Who are we? Again, what am I bringing to the relationship? As I understand self I understand more about what kind of boundaries are important to me. Anger is felt when boundaries are crossed.

I worked with a couple in which the husband's behavior sent the message that his wife should be there to meet all of his relational/social needs. The wife felt tremendous pressure. She was holding this pressure inside rather than sharing with him what she felt and that she could not do this for him. She needed to set a boundary. We are able to set boundaries when we are aware of what we are uncomfortable with that our spouse may be asking us to do. This may be in the sexual realm, the relational/social realm, the marriage role realm. The ability to say no in gentle ways is intimate.

Christ desires us to become one, but He never said become enmeshed. The more I become intimate with Gary—trusting him, being honest with him, allowing him to see me as myself, forgiving him, and setting boundaries—the more one I am with him because I know him and he knows me in deeper ways. At the same time in this oneness we also grow to become more unique! Much of what God created in my gifting is released and people see Gary and me as one, but they also see how we are unique and complement each other.

Setting boundaries and talking about boundaries is a part of this oneness process and key to feeling safe with our partner. When we say no, I can't go to a movie tonight, or this is not a good time to talk about the too-large phone bill, or I would love to work on that remodeling project with you or go on that speaking engagement, but I just don't have the energy for it right now, we risk being intimate. As we say no we say I trust you to hold my boundary with care. When our spouse sets a boundary, we must make an effort not to take it personally and to keep ourselves from crossing it. It's important to recognize our spouse's need for the limit.

Intimacy—so vital, so central, so misunderstood, so rarely experienced in the way that God desired for us to experience. There is hope though! Intimacy can be understood, it can be grown from little, and it can be restored.

Now that we've examined the components to intimacy, in the next chapter we'll look at some of the barriers that keep us from achieving the intimacy we so long for.

SMALL BEGINNINGS

1. Write your own definition of intimacy and talk about it with your spouse.
2. What key component (self, trust, honesty, forgiveness, boundaries) do you believe you hear God calling you to invest your energy in just a little bit more to improve the intimacy level in your relationship? What key component do you believe you and your spouse are experiencing that is helpful for your relationship?
3. When you were/are "mad about us" or madly in love with your spouse, what is going on between the two of you that affects these positive feelings?
4. What holds you back from risking intimacy?
5. What might be some possible ways to improve intimacy in your marriage even in the next couple of weeks?

BARRIERS TO INTIMACY

John and Sarah have been married for thirty-some years. Like so many couples, after walking through many life experiences together and developing certain patterns, they have come to believe that things will never change. John carries with him a "Sarah filter" through which he sees her that says she always reacts and responds in a particular way. John believes that Sarah does not hear his heart, that she only cares about what he should hear and understand about her. He asks himself, *Can she really love me, or will I continue to feel criticized and like a failure at meeting her needs?* Sarah sees John and longs for connection. She wants him to see her heart and to demonstrate tenderness and love rather than distant and cold disapproval. This couple is stuck in seeing each other and experiencing each other from one perspective. They have an invisible barrier between them because of their negative views of each other. This can be a huge barrier to intimacy for a couple.

We discussed in the previous chapter what intimacy is made of and what grows intimacy between two people. In this chapter we will take a closer look at some of the barriers to intimacy. We often feel that we want intimacy and we may have an idea of what it takes to grow it.

But do we understand how to identify the barriers and prevent them from crushing the intimacy we signed up for when we said "I do"? We may even feel that our spouse doesn't want intimacy with us. Perhaps we have grown angry and we have even communicated rejection toward our spouse. That is a fairly large barrier right there!

WHAT IS A BARRIER?

A barrier is something that blocks, prevents, or obstructs. A barrier is any obstacle to the very love and intimacy that we want. In the last chapter we named the many parts that play into growing intimacy, such as building trust, being vulnerable, spending time together, bringing a sense of self to the relationship, being honest, forgiving, and setting realistic boundaries. Other contributors to growing intimacy are communicating well, understanding differences, navigating conflict, growing sexually, and so on.

A barrier's job is to prevent moving through. As long as the barrier is in place we will not move through it to the intimacy we say we want. Sometimes we don't even see the barrier right in front of us or know how we have contributed to it, let alone understand what it takes to remove the barrier.

For years I (Carrie) had not listened to Gary in ways that said I truly wanted to hear his heart. He had built a barrier around his heart because I had put up the roadblock of crummy listening. A few years ago we were flying to Oregon to present a marriage enrichment seminar. We were enjoying a lovely breakfast while sitting in the Denver airport waiting for our next flight when Gary turned to me to share his heart. He even used feeling words as he said, "I felt hurt last year when Nathan was a senior in high school that he didn't listen to me when I would give him advice. I will never have that time with him again, and it hurts that he did not want me to share with him." Instead of looking at Gary and communicating that I was glad he let me know how he was feeling and that I was sorry that he hurt, I moved into teaching, reprimanding, and advice mode. I told him that no teenage boy wants the advice of his father and that he should know that and not get so worked up about it. (It is embarrassing writing these words even now!)

It is important to understand that usually lurking right behind any barrier is anger stemming from some type of hurt, fear, or frustration. Whether Gary was right or wrong about what he had tried to accomplish with Nathan was not the point. The point was that I had the opportunity to really listen with my heart to his heart and become close to him in his feelings and I did not do that. I affirmed what he had been feeling for some time in our marriage—that it was not safe for him to really share his feelings. This was a barrier that created some anger in Gary out of his hurt and frustration with me. Fortunately that morning he shared that experience and I finally got it. I let the walls of my defensiveness come down and I asked for forgiveness for not seeing how I was shutting him out. It only took twenty years to get to that revelation! We hope you get it before we did!

STRONG INTIMACY BARRIERS

NEGATIVE PERSPECTIVE OF SPOUSE

Dr. John Gottman, a leading marriage and parenting researcher, found that the number one predictor of whether a couple would go down the road toward divorce or not was whether they thought negatively or positively toward each other. Assuming the worst about our spouse can penetrate into all realms of who they are and how we interact with them.

If I think that Gary is generally unkind, not gentle, thoughtless, and insensitive, then I will not believe that he has good things for me, I will not take criticism from him, and I will not want to go through conflict. Assuming the worst about our spouse can become a habit and can start soon after we marry. It can be as small as believing they do not love and care for us as much as they should. If they forget to take the trash out it is because they are only thinking of themselves; if they are late without calling they do not care enough to do so; if they do not want sex as much it must be because they do not desire us as much as they used to.

Some of these issues may need some attention and some of them may be true. But in Gottman's research, in our work with couples, and in our own marriage, we've found that thinking negatively about our spouse can become a habit and is a very strong barrier to creating safety and intimacy.

When I think Gary does not think positively about me, then I do not want to trust him with my heart. In fact, I may spend much of my time defending my heart. This, with time, creates anger at him. Many of us do not realize that it is a choice to view our spouse positively. We can assume the best about our spouse until proven differently. An occupational hazard of being human is to think negatively about ourselves and others. As we choose to believe the best, we can make a powerful difference in the level of trust and intimacy we will experience in our relationships.

In the example I used earlier of John and Sarah's marriage, we saw that they had created negative filters through which they were seeing each other. When John would look at Sarah, he put on his negative Sarah lenses, and Sarah viewed John through her negative John lenses. When we do this we seldom can point out any positive and helpful action, reaction, word, emotion, etc., that our spouse has to offer. Because we have been hurt or frustrated or angry with our spouse without understanding or resolving issues, these experiences color anything good or positive or helpful about our spouse.

John asks Sarah to go to dinner on Thursday night. Instead of saying, "That would be lovely; where shall we go?" she responds by saying, "Oh, you're just asking me out because you haven't done so in a month and you feel guilty or you are doing it because our counselor said we needed to have more dating experiences. You are not asking me out because you want to be with me." See how this negativity totally sabotages anything good about what John has done and ultimately sabotages a good time for Sarah?

INABILITY TO UNDERSTAND AND AFFIRM DIFFERENCES

Many people act as if everyone else should be exactly like them! We marry because we like the unique things about our spouse that are different from us. I liked that Gary had an abundance of energy, that he had great vision and initiative. I liked that he was a man! I did not know that after we were married some of these things would be terribly annoying! Differences become barriers when we become critical of each other and how we are different. Some things we may need to negotiate, but other things we can come to accept and perhaps even appreciate about our spouse.

When we travel Gary likes to take in all that he can from a place that he visits. He likes to find the museums, understand the history, and enjoy all the things the area has to offer. On the island of Maui in Hawaii, one can take a helicopter ride, scuba dive, drive to Hana, bike ride down Haleakala Crater, wind surf, walk the city of Lahina— well, you get the picture. Gary would be the type who would want to do all of that on a first trip to Maui. I might want to try a couple of those things, but other than that I would love playing in the ocean, sun tanning, snorkeling, shopping a little, enjoying fine food, resting, reading, and going for walks. Instead of putting each other down for who we are, we have learned to find out what is important to both of us. When we're on vacation we decide what we want to do together, what we will do apart, and what we are willing to give up for the relationship.

We don't have to let our differences be a determiner of who is right or wrong or something that divides us. Oh, the hurt and frustration that can build from differences! Women can feel unloved if their husbands do not want to have long, drawn-out conversations with them on a frequent basis. Yet most men are not built to desire these types of interactions, even though they may pull it off during the dating period.

According to Pat Love and Steven Stosny in their book *How to Improve Your Marriage Without Talking About It*, men will often, once they're married, perceive their home as a safe place to just be quiet. They no longer have to talk about everything, and that feels good to them! Women often see it differently. For most women coming into marriage is even more opportunity for verbal connection. Most women desire to connect through talking, using feeling words and communicating needs. They have an innate desire to bond, and bonding often takes place through talking. If a woman's husband is silent, she might believe he is upset with her or feel that her husband is cold and distant. But often husbands who get quiet with their wives feel safe and have a sense of contentment. Who says it is more right to talk a lot! In intimate marriages honesty, vulnerability, and conflict resolution can take place with few words, especially when we come to trust and understand each other.

What is important here is to see that differences in our gender, our personality, and our cultural background can be strong barriers to knowing each other and experiencing the level of intimacy we want. We must learn what our differences are and then have a love and tolerance for these differences.

LACK OF EMPATHY

There is a relatively new field of study called emotional intelligence. Research is beginning to demonstrate that emotional intelligence—our ability to understand our emotions, express them, and understand emotions in others—may be a greater predictor of whether we will be successful in life than our IQ. Empathy is one of the most important and valuable relationship skills in the study of emotional intelligence. Stosny and Love actually say that developing the skill of seeing the world through your partner's eyes, while holding on to your own perspective, may be the single most important skill in intimate relationships.[1]

Empathy is the ability to feel some of what our spouse is feeling as they look at their world. It is not hard to imagine that if we cannot see things just a little from each other's perspective then we will not be able to know each other.

Intimacy requires that we know each other more deeply with time. Both men and women struggle with this skill. One might think women are better at it, and perhaps they are. But most of the husbands I work with do not feel that their wives see their world through their eyes. They see their wives as having compassion for their kids, for their friends, and for animals, but when it comes to his heart, the wife goes someplace else. Usually she goes to how he has hurt her or does not understand her. She is assuming the worst. She gets critical and then he gets defensive, and off the couple goes, never experiencing the very thing they long for.

They both are saying, "Just know me. Please look through my eyes for just a few moments and experience my world: It gets hard sometimes. It is hard worrying about whether I will be able to raise these children to be responsible adults; it is hard going to work each day and dealing with the people there, and I want you to know that." For Gary and me it is hard walking the cancer journeys we have each walked, and we cannot assume that each person's journey is the same, because it's not.

In the movie *The Story of Us,* the viewer just knows that the characters played by Bruce Willis and Michelle Pfeiffer are going to get a divorce. They fight and struggle and work hard at hurting each other, but they do not have a clue as to how to see the world from each other's eyes until the very end of the movie. They begin to wander over to the other set of eyes before them and risk looking from behind them and feeling the hurt in the heart of their spouse, perhaps for the first time in years. It is at this point that they decide not to divorce, that they have built way too much history with each other, and that they might possibly be able to change the negative parts of the history to positive and build the intimacy with each other that they crave.

In the movie Michelle's character is structured, detailed, organized and Bruce's character is playful, spontaneous, unstructured. She feels very annoyed with him most of the time in the marriage, as if his personality is communicating to her that she is not important by not upholding her rules around the house, being willing to get things fixed, and following through on things she has asked him to do. He feels she has no ability to play with him, to enjoy being together, to laugh and be silly. In the movie they are going to tell their children after they pick them up from camp that they are getting a divorce. Bruce is driving and she notices once again that the gas tank is close to empty and the washer fluid in the car has dried up, excellent examples of his lack of follow-through. More ways that he says, "I don't care about you." She almost starts to criticize him for his behavior when she has a look of "aha" on her face, and she chooses to not address the low gas tank and wiper fluid. Instead she says something connecting to him like "How are you doing right now?" She gets it for the first time that her way is not the only way of viewing the world but that her husband views it very different and in that difference he still has value. Her heart begins to turn.

LACK OF SEXUAL INTERACTION

Most of us would agree that this area of lack of sexual interaction or the inability to get on the same page sexually can be a big barrier to intimacy. It is our premise that most couples that are having trouble in other areas of the relationship will have trouble here as well. Being vulnerable sexually requires the feelings of safety and trust. To experience optimal spiritual oneness, husbands and wives will need to see each other from a positive perspective and be able to accept and navigate differences.

Many of the barriers for building intimacy are barriers for building sexual intimacy as well, and sexual intimacy is needed to build overall intimacy. We build barriers in our sexual experience when we don't talk about sex and when we don't take responsibility for our needs in our sexual interaction with our spouse. We need to have fun with sex, and sex can be both routine and spontaneous. Having it is important! Often breaking down barriers in other areas of the relationship will enable this area of the relationship to grow.

EXPRESSING EMOTIONS IN INAPPROPRIATE WAYS

In truth this book is about this barrier! The unhealthy expression of anger and other emotions can run down intimacy very quickly. If I rant and rave and have a temper tantrum, get hysterical, yell, etc., then I quickly become an unsafe person for Gary and myself. I probably don't even understand what is going on inside if I am just doing emotional dumping. Most anger that is not expressed in helpful ways ends up being destructive and a roadblock to intimacy. Notice we are not saying that anger needs to be eliminated, but rather it needs to be identified, understood, dealt with, and expressed in helpful ways. Emotional intimacy is so important to the foundation of trust. As I experience my own emotions, identify them, and express them to Gary, he knows a core part of who I am that he cannot know unless I do this in healthy ways. In the next chapter we'll talk about emotions and how to identify and express them.

To experience intimacy we must notice if we have a reactive spirit or a responsive spirit. For years I was very reactive. Gary could have a look on his face or a tone in his voice and I would let that get me going. I would accuse him of being angry at me, I would get defensive, and then this behavior would almost always escalate the situation rather than be helpful. I did not take the time to listen, to discover what was really going on, or to notice my own emotions in the process. A responsive spirit desires to understand and seeks to be empathetic. As I am empathetic to what is going on for Gary I get out of myself, out of my reactions, and I am much more able to hear what is going on for him. He will then probably be much more able to hear what is going on for me.

Actually, when I would get real reactive and raise my voice, Gary started leaving the room until I was able to calm down. I appreciate that he was able to do that. Now I will take myself away to calm down or he will take himself away for a timeout to calm down if he needs to. Timeouts are so important when we need time to understand what we are thinking and feeling and find healthy ways to communicate these things to our spouse. Anger and erratically expressed emotions can be a tremendous barrier to safety, trust, and intimacy.

WAITING FOR YOUR PARTNER TO CHANGE

Intimacy can begin right away in a marriage, and barriers can begin to come down if even one person makes a decision to do something differently. In my work with couples often one spouse comes in and says, "I've tried everything to improve my marriage and now I am ready to try counseling." What most of them are really saying is that they have tried everything to get their spouse to change in order to meet their needs. I know this may strike a nerve. Hang in there for a moment, don't go away. If we are brutally honest, we have to admit that we are like this as humans. We read marriage books and see what we need to do differently, and we may even do some of those things. But with time if our spouse does not read the book or does not cooperate in the way we think they should, we get mad at them! They are in trouble and we are disappointed.

We have a choice though. We can choose to radically change whether our partner decides to change or not. Radical means we truly become committed to being healthy in the way we come to our world, to being a person that is safe to be around, emotionally aware, and empathetic. We can strive to understand our anger and express it in helpful ways.

What motivates us to want to change even though our spouse doesn't seem to want to? Honestly, it is a broken heart for Christ. A few years ago Christ got a hold of me as I was writing a paper for a Denver Seminary class on the Sermon on the Mount. I started reading these Scriptures and I asked myself, *Do I really hunger and thirst after righteousness, and if I did wouldn't I really act differently?*

We are motivated to change by allowing Christ to be the center of our heart! The center cannot be whether our spouse loves us like we want, or whether we are getting our needs met. We are motivated to change when we understand that each day is a new day to walk with Christ and to please Him with our heart, our words, our actions, and who we are in general. Yes, couples change at a faster pace when both are getting it and are desiring to improve or be Christlike. But truly much can change when one person makes a choice to change and be more Christlike in the marriage. It takes lots of courage to do this! One of my favorite Scriptures as I walk with cancer comes from Joshua 1:9, "Be strong and courageous. . . . For the Lord your God will be with you wherever you go."

DO SOMETHING DIFFERENT

We thirst for intimacy because our worlds are so dry of love and deep relationships. We may not break down every barrier or roadblock to intimacy right away, but some will have influence over the others. A decision by one spouse to change may be enough to have a great impact on the level of intimacy and how we deal with anger. Each day on this earth is another opportunity to do something different from the day before. That is encouraging news!

SMALL BEGINNINGS

1. What are some barriers to intimacy in your marriage, either ones we mentioned or others you can identify?

2. How are they barriers? What would be different if the barriers were broken down?

3. What might your spouse say would be a barrier or barriers to intimacy?

4. If you were to make a choice as to a change you would like to make in order to walk just a little more closely with Christ, what would that be? How would it influence your marriage?

CHAPTER

4

THE EMOTIONAL SIDE OF INTIMACY

I've come to see that I'm afraid of my feelings," Brad said softly. After a long pause he added, "I don't know who I am emotionally, and it scares me to death. I don't think I even know how or what to feel." Brad had grown up in an alcoholic home. His father's drinking binges and periods of unemployment kept the family on an emotional roller coaster and in a state of almost constant instability. As the oldest child it had been Brad's job to protect his mother and his brothers and sisters. Although he wasn't consciously aware of it, he had become the hero of the family.

For seven years Brad had been the successful pastor of a large evangelical church. He prided himself on how hard he worked and on how much of his time was spent serving the Lord. If you had talked with him two years earlier, he would have told you that he had the perfect marriage, the perfect family, and the perfect ministry.

But then his children started going through adolescence. His wife, Karen, began to be more assertive about her frustration with their lack of meaningful communication and intimacy. He began to lose his enthusiasm and intensity for ministry. He found himself becoming frustrated at little things that never would have bothered him before.

He became more and more negative and critical and found himself face-to-face with a dimension of his life he had worked hard to ignore. He was a wounded healer who had no idea how to understand, let alone deal with his own pain.

If you had talked with Karen two years earlier she would have told you that their marriage was anything but perfect. They had little one-on-one time, few deep discussions, and little physical intimacy. Most of their communication centered around the church and the kids, and somewhere along the line they had lost any meaningful sense of being a couple. Much of Karen's hurt and frustration came from the fact that Brad seemed oblivious to this, and the more she communicated her frustration to him the more he would withdraw into his church world.

In Karen's home emotions were rarely discussed. She never heard her parents say "I love you" and doesn't remember seeing them demonstrate any love to each other. The only display of emotions she had any memory of was hearing her parents yelling at each other behind closed doors. This was usually followed by several days of her parents' not talking to each other. "In my family it wasn't okay to express feelings, but somehow that made me even more aware of my own feelings. I became known as the emotional one of the family."

But while it wasn't okay for Karen to express her feelings, she learned to rely on her feelings for survival. She learned how to read her parents' tones of voice and other nonverbal expressions to know when it was and wasn't safe to join in the conversation and when she needed to disappear to avoid the fireworks.

As an adult, she was respected for her unselfishness and her servant heart. However, during the past six months Karen had become aware of increasing feelings of bitterness and resentment. She found herself withdrawing from usual activities and avoiding people. In the past two months she had to fight off feelings of wanting to tell people off, especially Brad. Up to now she had been able to handle the bitterness and resentment, but she could no longer sit on the pain and ignore the loneliness and isolation of a bankrupt marriage relationship.

Brad and Karen came to counseling seeking help for their marriage. They were aware that the way they were expressing their anger was a problem. But the root problem was not their anger. The root problem was that neither one of them understood, valued, or knew how to deal with their emotions.

Somewhere along the line they decided that feelings weren't important. Brad and Karen stopped listening to their feelings and tried to make them disappear. They both pursued excellence in serving others. When you are busy taking care of everyone else, you don't have time to be aware of what is taking place in your own life. Busyness can be an effective yet short-term anesthetic for painful emotions.

MADE IN GOD'S IMAGE— EMOTIONS INCLUDED

It doesn't take newlyweds long to discover that the precious intimacy they thought would come easily can be quickly broken. They bump into differences of opinion, different personality preferences, expectations, and emotional land mines they didn't know existed or chose to ignore during their dating and courtship. Brad and Karen began their marriage madly in love and mad about each other, but now as they talked about their marriage they were just plain mad. And neither one really understood why.

We have emotions because God has emotions and we are made in His image. Emotions are *intended* by God, *designed* by God, and *created* by God to enrich and enhance our lives, to be a potentially powerful and positive force for good. Emotions enhance our ability to be in relationship with Him and with one another. But due to the fall and the effects of sin in our lives, our emotions, like our minds and our wills, have become damaged and distorted. For many, the emotions that God gave to make life more meaningful instead make life more miserable.

Emotions are important. The Bible has a lot to say about emotions.

49

From Genesis through Revelation we read about God's emotions and the emotions of men and women He created. In the New Testament we find that Christ experienced and expressed a wide range of emotions, including love, compassion, joy, fear, sorrow, disappointment, frustration, rejection, loneliness, and anger.

Our emotions influence almost every aspect of our lives. God speaks to us through our emotions. They are like a sixth sense. Emotions help us to monitor our needs, make us aware of good and evil, and provide motivation and energy for growth and change. Emotions give us the vigor, force, power, and impetus for living. Emotions are energy in motion.

UNHEALTHY RESPONSES TO EMOTIONS

Sin has led to one of two unhealthy ways to deal with our emotions. The first is to deny or *ignore* them. This was Brad's characteristic response. From this perspective the intellectual side is more important than the emotional. Emotions are at best unimportant and at worst a mark of immaturity. Unfortunately when we ignore or minimize the emotional realities of our life it distorts our perspective and leads us to distrust our experience. We often tend to deny or ignore the very things God wants to use to help us grow.

The second unhealthy pattern is to allow ourselves to be *controlled* by our emotions. This is an equally dangerous position and the one that reflected Karen's approach. From this perspective the intellect is suspect. If you don't feel it then you can't trust it. Karen had grown up with an oversensitivity to emotions and functioned as if her feelings were facts that needed to be acted upon. Sometimes her feelings were accurate, but other times they weren't. At times this blind faith in her feelings caused her to misinterpret and overreact to situations in ways that only made matters worse.

By God's grace there is a third option. The only healthy response is to choose to view our emotions from God's perspective and to bring them into harmony with our minds. True maturity involves a balance between our heart and our head and our will—between our feeling, our thinking, and our doing. Each one is important. Each one was designed by God for our good. Each one is a manifestation of the image of God in us and plays a vital role in healthy relationships.

Both Brad and Karen realized that they had brought a lot of emotional baggage into their marriage that had little to do with each other and a lot to do with what they had learned growing up. These unhealthy emotional patterns had taken a toll on them as individuals and were now threatening their marriage. The unhealthy anger that they had worked so hard to manage had eroded the dreams they had brought into their marriage and was now starting to threaten the survival of their relationship.

CHRISTIANS STRUGGLE WITH EMOTIONS

Jesus shed His blood on the cross to save us from the consequences of our sins and to give us eternal life. Christ sent the Holy Spirit to indwell us and help us "become conformed to the image of His Son" (Romans 8:29 NKJV). Christ died to make a difference in our lives. Unfortunately for some Christians, the difference is primarily external or at best intellectual. We are still influenced by old thought patterns and controlled by our emotions. Our lives are sometimes dominated by fear, hurt, frustration, anger, or depression.

We can get discouraged and feel guilty because we still have those struggles. This creates a problem. Do we share our questions and struggles with others and risk appearing immature and unspiritual? Or do we deny our problems and pretend that everything is going great? Rather than risk the humiliation and possible rejection that might come from sharing our feelings, many of us ignore our problems and stuff our emotions. But eventually this creates an even greater problem. We can only pretend for so long.

Although they had been married for many years, Karen found that it was still difficult for her to be transparent and to risk being vulnerable with Brad. "Although Brad had committed his life to me 'until death do us part,' it was still hard for me to risk his disapproval and rejection. It was harder for me than I had ever thought it would be."

When we ask Christ into our heart, there is a radical transformation that takes place. At the same time, the consequences of sin on our mind, will, emotions, and relationships does not immediately disappear. We believe that an important part of the process of sanctification involves the healing of our damaged emotions, which frees us to love and trust in ways that lead to the intimacy we all long for. As you'll see in this book, God has designed the marriage relationship to be one of the main places where this healing takes place.

It's impossible to cultivate deep levels of intimacy without a basic understanding of emotions. Over the years we've discovered that unless we understand what emotions are, where they come from, why God gave them to us, and how they function we will have only limited success in healing those damaged emotions and overcoming the barriers that keep us from knowing and being known, from experiencing our marriage as a safe haven and from experiencing the deep levels of trust and intimacy that God designed for us in our marriage relationship.

WHAT EXACTLY ARE EMOTIONS?

We've asked this question of numerous groups, and the most common response is "Emotions are what I feel." That's true—many people use feelings and emotions interchangeably. Yet it doesn't give us a definition. It's somewhat like trying to define air by saying, "Air is what I breathe." Most people are surprised that something as common as emotions can be so difficult to define.

Webster's defines *emotion* as "a psychic and physical reaction subjectively experienced as strong feeling and physiologically involving changes that prepare the body for immediate vigorous action." The word *emotion* is derived from the Latin word *emovare*, which means "to move" or having to do with motion, movement, and energy. I heard one speaker say that emotion should be spelled e-motion since emotions are energy in motion.

Emotions are the "motivating forces of our lives, driving us to go ahead, pushing us backward, stopping us completely, determining what we do, how we feel, what we want, and whether we get what we want. Our hates, loves, fears, and what to do about them are determined by our emotional structure. There is nothing in our lives that does not have the emotional factor as its mainspring. It gives us power, or makes us weak, operates for our benefit or to our detriment, for our happiness or confusion."[1]

What are some of the most common emotions? In seminars and workshops I (Gary) have asked participants to make a list of frequently experienced emotions. The lists that various groups have come up with have had as few as 11 and as many as 82 different examples of what they considered emotions. (It's interesting to note that the group that came up with only 11 was a group of men and the group that came up with 82 was a group of women.) Some of the emotions that are most frequently listed include

accepted	excited	lonely
angry	fearful	loved
anxious	frightened	pleased
appreciated	frustrated	proud
bored	generous	sad
concerned	glad	scared
confident	grieving	shame
confused	happy	surprised
delighted	humiliated	terrified
depressed	hurt	uncomfortable
elated	indifferent	unsure
embarrassed	jealous	worried

CHARACTERISTICS OF EMOTIONS

One of the most helpful ways to understand emotions is to look at some characteristics that emotions have in common.

EVERYONE EXPERIENCES EMOTIONS

Joe was a tall and athletic man in his mid-fifties. He had grown up on the Sand Hills of western Nebraska and had been a cattle rancher all of his life. When he came into my office the first thing he said was, "I want you to know that I'm just not an emotional kind of guy." He went on to explain that some people, especially women, have a lot of emotions and some people don't. He was convinced that he was someone who didn't have or need many emotions. That stoic philosophy had worked for most of his life. However, when land prices fell and he found out that his wife had cancer, his emotion-free world began to crumble, and he discovered that he didn't have the resources to deal with all of his newly discovered emotions.

Here's the deal. Some people are more aware of their emotions than others, but the experience of emotions isn't optional. Regardless of gender, age, race, or socioeconomic level, emotions are an integral part of our standard equipment. The only thing that's optional is how we choose to express them. I can't always choose what I'm going to feel. But I can choose how long I feel it. With God's help we can change our emotional pattern.

EMOTIONS AREN'T GOOD OR BAD, RIGHT OR WRONG

This is one of the most important aspects of emotions to remember. There aren't any good or bad, healthy or unhealthy emotions. However, it is possible for emotions to have a good or bad, healthy or unhealthy effect on our lives. The degree to which we understand the role that emotions play in our lives will to a great degree determine their effect on us.

For example, most people view love as a positive emotion. However, when we allow love to get out of control or attach love to the wrong person or thing it can blind us to reality and have a devastating effect. For example, narcissism involves an immature, self-centered, and inordinate love of self that narrows our world and limits our ability to grow.

Anger is usually viewed as a negative emotion. When anger is out of control it can cause irreparable damage. But the emotion of anger provides a source of power that can be used for good or for evil. It can be constructive or destructive. In this book you will see that when we understand our anger and choose to express it in healthy kinds of ways, it has enormous potential for good.

WE CAN HAVE STRONG EMOTIONS AND NOT BE AWARE OF THEM

One of the psychological tests we use in our center has a scale that measures anger. When Brad took this test he scored 96 out of a possible 100 points. When I started to discuss this with him he interrupted and in a loud voice stated, "These test results are wrong. I am not an angry man!" The expression on Karen's face told me different. Brad had no idea the degree to which his unhealthy anger had become a problem. In fact, it was difficult for him to even admit the possibility that he was at times dominated by his anger.

EMOTIONS HAVE A PHYSICAL EFFECT

When we experience our emotions there are changes in our central nervous system that involve chemicals and neurotransmitters. There are also changes in our peripheral nervous system. When we experience an emotion our heart may beat faster, the pupils in our eyes may dilate, we may have increased perspiration, we may tremble, tears may come to our eyes, we may get goose bumps, we may experience a tremendous surge of energy, or we may feel totally drained.

MOST EMOTIONAL RESPONSES ARE LEARNED

Different people can have different emotional responses to the same event. The emotion we experience is to a great degree determined by the meaning or interpretation we make of that event. What excites and energizes one person can bring panic and emotional paralysis to another. There are several factors that influence our emotional responses, including childhood experiences, where we were raised, our spiritual background, and our personality type.

One of the most important factors is our home environment. Some of us grew up in homes such as the one described by Karen at the beginning of this chapter. These were homes in which emotions weren't modeled or discussed. The few emotions that were expressed were kept behind closed doors. There were no names given to them and no healthy opportunities for understanding them.

There are others like Brad who grew up in homes where emotions were not merely ignored. Emotional expression was punished and emotional repression was reinforced. Those of us raised in this environment quickly learned that it wasn't safe to feel. For the sake of survival we were trained to ignore emotions or filter them out, or when one accidentally crept up to the surface, stuff it back down.

We weren't free to learn how to experience or express our God-given emotions. The only thing that felt safe was not to feel. We became emotionally numb. Now, as adults, we are faced with the task of unlearning old dysfunctional patterns and replacing them with healthy new patterns. But that task is easier said than done.

IF WE DON'T UNDERSTAND AND CONTROL OUR EMOTIONS THEY WILL CONTROL US

Several years ago I had the opportunity to speak to a group of mothers of preschoolers. They had asked me to talk about emotions. When I stated that it is important for us to understand and control our emotions, one woman took offense and raised her hand to disagree. She interpreted my use of the term *control* to mean that we should ignore our emotions and keep them under control. I thanked her for giving me the opportunity to make an important clarification.

For the person who wants to be healthy and mature, ignoring

emotions is not an option. It can take an enormous amount of energy to ignore your emotions. And even then we can't ignore them indefinitely. Emotional repression eventually leads to self-destructive behaviors and addictions such as overworking, overeating, eating too little, alcohol and drug dependence, compulsive spending, sexual addictions, controlling behaviors, and other compulsive patterns.

The word *control* means to guide or manage and can refer to the skill involved in using a tool. The professional craftsman has a variety of tools in his tool chest. It takes time and effort to learn how to effectively and safely use those tools. Some tools are more necessary and effective in some situations and totally ineffective or useless in others. The effectiveness of the tool also depends on the skill of the craftsman.

Our emotions are like tools. It takes time and effort to learn about our emotions. Through trial and error we learn when we can trust our emotions and when we can't. When I talk about controlling our emotions I'm talking about increasing our skills in understanding our emotions and then managing how we choose to express them. Healthy people are aware of their emotions. They are more likely to understand themselves and more accurately perceive the feelings of others.

SHARED EMOTIONS ARE THE CURRENCY OF INTIMATE RELATIONSHIPS

A growing body of medical and relational research is telling us that to a great degree emotions are how we know ourselves and know others. Unfortunately many of us don't know how to share our emotions in healthy ways. Brad had years of seminary training on how to communicate his ideas with clarity, yet precious little training in clearly communicating his feelings.

The deeper the emotion the more difficult it is to share. We may cry at the wrong time, laugh at the wrong time, or get angry at the wrong time. When we do try to share our emotions with our spouse, we may come on too strong or not strong enough. We might get embarrassed. Our spouse could misunderstand. We sometimes decide it's safer not to risk the humiliation of being rejected or laughed at so we don't share.

God designed our emotions to help us understand ourselves and others. This is especially true in the marriage relationship. When we express our emotions we have the opportunity to confirm or disconfirm what we are feeling. When we conceal our emotions they become more complex and difficult for us to understand. Withholding our emotions can distort our view of the world, isolate us from others, and cause us to remain strangers even to those we love the most. When we don't share our emotions, others don't know what is most important to us.

Emotions were made to be expressed. They are the language of healthy marriages, families, and friendships. They provide the passion and intensity needed to initiate and sustain a healthy marriage. In his classic book *Why Am I Afraid to Tell You Who I Am?* John Powell says, "I can only know that much of myself which I have had the courage to confide to you."[2] When we express our emotions it helps us and our loved ones better understand who we are and what is important to us.

The degree to which our emotions help us or hinder us depends on the degree to which we acknowledge them, understand them, choose to channel them through our prayer life and thought life, and view them from a balanced, healthy perspective. In marriage it's especially important to acknowledge and understand our anger. In the next chapter we'll share a healthy perspective on this often misunderstood emotion.

SMALL BEGINNINGS

1. Thank God for making you in His image. Thank Him for your mind, your will, and your emotions.
2. Ask God to help you better understand the role of emotions in

becoming a mature man or woman.

3. Examine what the Bible has to say about emotions. Look at the life of David and note the role of emotions in his life. As you read through the gospels examine the life of Christ. What kinds of emotions did He experience and how did He choose to express them?

4. What did you learn about emotions from the way you were raised?

5. How has your attitude toward emotions affected your marriage?

6. Observe your own emotional pattern.

   •• What emotions do you frequently experience?

   •• What are the emotions that you rarely experience?

   •• What emotions are easy for you to express?

   •• What emotions are difficult for you to express?

   •• What aspect of your emotional pattern would you like to change?

7. Pick one emotion you want to understand better and that you believe God would have you develop more effective skills in expressing.

   •• Define that emotion.

   •• Make a list of what you consider to be unhealthy and healthy expressions of that emotion.

   •• Are there any models from Scripture of healthy expressions of that emotion?

   •• What are three specific ways you can begin to change your response pattern?

   •• Ask your spouse and two or three same-sex friends to pray for this specific area in your life.

CHAPTER
5

FROM INTIMACY
TO ANGER

One of the joys of having young children is that it gave us the opportunity to read what many consider children's stories. When our youngest son, Andrew, was three, his favorite story was *Make Way for Ducklings*. One night after a long day of counseling I (Gary) found myself reading the story, again, and I came across a part that reminded me of a couple I had seen that same day.

Mr. and Mrs. Mallard were looking for a place to live. But it seems that every time Mr. Mallard saw what he thought would be a great place to live, Mrs. Mallard said it was no good. She was worried that there might be foxes in the woods or turtles lurking in the water. Being a concerned parent, she was not about to raise a family where there might be foxes or turtles. So they flew on and on.[1]

Can you visualize Mr. and Mrs. Mallard flying around, looking for a place to raise a family? They are two very different ducks that met somewhere, fell in love, and decided that life would be happier together than apart. However, early in their relationship they have already discovered that they have different tastes, preferences, and opinions. It seems as if every time Mr. Mallard discovers a nice place to live, Mrs. Mallard disagrees. The implication is that she is a more concerned parent than he is, so he gives in, and in deference to her wishes they fly on to another area.

Now, if this story were about humans and not ducks, this seemingly innocuous discussion would probably end in a fight: "You never like what I like." "Well, that's because you have such lousy taste." "What do you mean by that?" "You know exactly what I mean by that." "Well, your mother doesn't have such great taste either." "What does my mother have to do with it?" And so on and so on.

Earlier in the day I had met with a couple who were mad at each other and experiencing serious marital problems. Steve and Jane had been married only six months and they were already bumping into each other's differences. Like Mr. and Mrs. Mallard, one of their differences involved trying to decide where they should live.

"I don't understand how he could change in such a short time!" Jane exclaimed. "While we were dating Steve talked a lot and seemed to enjoy being with friends. But since we've been married he has clammed up. He rarely wants to go out, and when he does go to a social function he always wants to come home early. Sometimes I feel like I married a hermit."

Steve, as you might guess, painted a much different picture. "I'm with people all day, and I look forward to coming home and just being with Jane." Steve continued, "It seems that if we're not talking all of the time something is drastically wrong and suddenly I'm a failure as a husband."

Not only were they having serious disagreements about the quantity of their communication, they were also going head to head over where to live. Before they were married they had decided that after the wedding Jane would move into Steve's apartment and they would begin saving money to purchase a home.

However, three months into the marriage Steve's accountant informed him that it would be in their best interest financially to purchase a home. Steve had looked around and found several (or so he thought) dream homes. However, each time he showed one to Jane, she invariably found several things wrong with it.

"Before we got married I never dreamed that we'd have arguments over such seemingly little things," Jane said. "It all seemed so much easier when we were just dating." I responded, "That's because it was easier." I assured Steve and Jane that they were not unique in the problems they were facing.

The marriage that they thought was made in heaven had become anything but heavenly. Unmet needs, unfulfilled expectations, and unrealized dreams had increased their disappointment with the relationship. Add a few misunderstandings and some miscommunication and they had the perfect recipe for irritation, frustration, and anger . . . everything except the intimacy they had expected and so desperately desired. The passion that in courtship expressed itself as mad *about* you became simply mad *at* you.

All they could see was that something was wrong, it didn't feel good, and they wanted it to stop. Like many couples, anger was an emotion that Steve and Jane knew very little about. They saw their disagreement as abnormal and unhealthy. What they didn't know was that they were in the process of taking one of the first steps on the road to developing a truly intimate relationship.

REAL LOVE INVOLVES
CONFLICT AND ANGER

One of the most devastating marital myths that cripples many relationships is that when two people are really in love with each other there will be few disagreements and virtually no conflict or anger. This sounds logical, but it just isn't true.

We've talked with many people who really believe that healthy couples don't have conflict or get angry. Now it is true that mannequins don't have conflict. It's also true that cadavers don't get angry. But real people in real relationships, who are actively working toward

63

figuring out what it means to become one while remaining individuals, experience disagreement, conflict, and anger.

The people to whom we give the most time and energy, in whom we invest the greatest amount of love and other emotions, are the ones we have the highest expectations of and are the ones with the greatest potential to trigger painful emotions such as fear, hurt, frustration, and eventually anger. Anger is not necessarily a sign of relational immaturity or instability. In fact, anger is an inherent component of all human relationships. But it is especially prevalent in romantic ones. The more dependent on someone and vulnerable you feel, the more likely they'll be the object of your anger as well as your affection.

Research tells us that happily married couples disagree and argue almost as much as unhappily married couples. The difference is whether they express their anger in healthy or unhealthy ways. The healthy expression of our anger can help us clarify, understand, and appreciate our differences. When we deny our anger and run from conflict we are running from the very process that God can use to heal our hurts and knit our hearts more tightly together in love.

Relationships that can't acknowledge or express appropriate anger are usually fragile, unstable, and anemic. When two people aren't secure in their love for each other, the marriage isn't strong enough to handle disagreement. This immaturity and insecurity lead to the chameleon syndrome: the tendency to be to the beholder whatever they think the beholder wants to see.

The long-term success of a relationship and the depth of intimacy a couple will experience depend on their willingness to find healthy ways for expressing and dealing with each other's emotions, and that includes the emotion of anger.

ANGER ISN'T ALWAYS NEGATIVE

Over the past twenty years we've led many marriage retreats dealing with the role of emotions in loving relationships. One of the emotions we discuss is anger. When we ask for a word association to anger the suggestions are invariably 99 percent negative. Clearly the vast majority of people view anger from a negative perspective. Both love and anger are emotions. Both love and anger were created by God. Both love and anger are talked about in God's Word. Yet love is viewed as a positive emotion and anger is viewed as a negative emotion.

CHARACTERISTICS OF ANGER

There are certain key characteristics of anger that are similar to the characteristics of all the emotions we discussed in the previous chapter. Understanding these characteristics is the first step in allowing God to help us use the emotion of anger in a constructive way in our marriage and family relationships and changing our view of anger from negative to positive. What are some of the core characteristics of anger we need to understand to help us make this emotion work for building greater intimacy in our marriage rather than working against it?

ANGER IS A GOD-GIVEN EMOTION

One of the core aspects of being a person is that we were created in God's image. Part of what it means to be made in God's image is that we, like God, have a variety of emotions. One of these emotions is anger. From Genesis 4:5 through Revelation 19:15, the Bible has a lot to say about anger. In fact, in the Old Testament alone anger is mentioned approximately 455 times with 375 of those passages referring to God's anger.

While the emotion of anger is not a sin, it is possible for us to respond to the emotion of anger in ways that lead to sin. The problem is not the emotion of anger but rather how we choose to express it. That is one reason why there are Scriptures in both the Old and New Testaments (Proverbs 16:32 and James 1:19) that admonish us to be slow to anger.

ANGER IS ONE OF THE MOST POWERFUL EMOTIONS

Anger is the most energizing of our emotions. Think about it. Worry, depression, fear, and grief drain us of energy. But when we experience the emotion of anger, adrenaline and noradrenaline are pumped into our central and peripheral nervous systems and our bodies go on alert. The emotion of anger can provide tremendous energy to deal with problems and change things for the good. But when we allow it to control us it can lead to destructive actions such as emotional, verbal, or even physical abuse and violence. Later in the book we're going to show you how to harness the energy of this powerful emotion to create understanding, increase safety, deepen trust, and develop the kind of intimacy that you long for in your marriage.

ANGER IS A SECONDARY EMOTION

Anger is usually the first emotion we see (even when others are present), and at that moment it's probably the only emotion that we are aware of. However—and this is very important—it is never the only emotion we have experienced. Just below the surface, out of our conscious awareness, there are almost always other, deeper emotions that need to be identified and acknowledged. Hidden deep underneath that secondary emotion of anger is usually some primary emotion such as fear, hurt, frustration, or sadness.

In Genesis 37, we find the well-known story of Joseph and his brothers. Joseph was one of the younger children in a family of twelve brothers. He was the favorite child. His father loved him more than all his brothers. His father, Jacob, paid special attention to him. He gave him special gifts. He honored him above the others.

This favoritism was blatant, and his brothers were hurt and jealous. They allowed their hurt and jealousy to turn into bitterness and resentment. When bitterness and resentment are allowed to smolder it doesn't take long for them to flare up into aggression and violence.

That's exactly what happened. In verse 18, we read that at first "they plotted against him to put him to death" (NASB). But Reuben talked them out of killing him. Instead, they sold him to a caravan of Ishmaelites for twenty shekels of silver, which is roughly equivalent to $18.75. Joseph was then taken to Egypt and sold to Potiphar, the captain of Pharaoh's bodyguard.

Was anger the first emotion that Joseph's brothers experienced? No! They first experienced feelings of hurt and rejection and jealousy. The anger came later. There are a wide range of emotions that might have come first. The emotions that most frequently precede anger are fear, hurt, or frustration. These initial feelings are often painful. Not only are they painful but they also can drain us of energy and increase our sense of vulnerability.

At an early age many of us learned that anger can divert our attention from these more painful emotions. If I get angry I can avoid or at least minimize my pain. Perhaps I can even influence or change the source of my anger. It doesn't take long to learn that it's easier to feel anger than it is to feel pain. Anger provides an increase of energy. It can decrease our sense of vulnerability and thus increase our sense of security.

ANGER WEARS MANY DISGUISES

Of all the emotions, anger is the one most likely to be disguised as something else. What are some of the most common disguises anger can take? When we begrudge, scorn, insult, and disdain others or when we are annoyed, offended, bitter, fed up, repulsed, irritated, infuriated, incensed, sarcastic, uptight, or cross, or when we experience frustration, indignation, exasperation, fury, wrath, or rage, we are probably experiencing some form of anger.

Anger can also manifest itself as criticism, silence, intimidation, hypochondria, numerous petty complaints, depression, gossip, sarcasm, blame, and passive-aggressive behaviors such as stubbornness, halfhearted efforts, forgetfulness, and laziness. When we learn to recognize the disguises of anger in ourselves and in our spouse we become much better equipped to deal with the cause of the anger and avoid the emotional explosions that can rock a relationship.

ANGER IS A FREQUENTLY EXPERIENCED EMOTION

Most of us experience the emotion of anger with greater frequency than we would like to admit. This is especially true if you have young children. From the number of times God's anger is mentioned in Scripture it is obvious that He also frequently experiences that emotion. We've seen several studies that suggest most people experience some form of anger at least eight to ten times a day. It may not always be identified as anger, but it is a form of anger.

UNHEALTHY ANGER CAN BE HARMFUL TO OTHERS

When people don't understand, listen to, and learn from their anger, it can become more intense and turn into rage. At this point they are faced with a much more dangerous problem. The energy of rage is much more powerful and much more difficult to direct than the energy of anger. If anger is ten thousand volts of energy, rage is one hundred thousand volts. When rage isn't dealt with, it can easily turn into aggression and then to violence. Some of the most devastating examples of violence occur between people who know and even love each other. I recently came across some sobering statistics that clearly demonstrate the potential harm of anger out of control:

- Every day in the U.S. four children die as a result of abuse by angry parents.[2]
- Most homicides are committed by people who know the victim.[3]
- Ten percent of all policemen killed are killed breaking up domestic arguments.[4]
- Every year millions of women are battered and bruised by raging husbands or boyfriends.[5]

UNHEALTHY ANGER CAN BE HAZARDOUS TO YOUR HEALTH

While the potentially harmful effect of anger on others is obvious, the harmful effects of anger on ourselves are a bit more subtle, but nonetheless real. An increasing amount of scientific evidence clearly suggests that the way in which we handle our emotions or allow them to handle us is a major factor in our physical well-being.

Occasional anger that is expressed in healthy ways is not harmful. In fact, learning how to express our anger in healthy ways can strengthen our health and increase our effectiveness. However, when anger is over-expressed or under-expressed for long periods of time, it keeps our body in a constant state of emergency. Chronic or sustained anger (unhealthy anger) increases blood pressure and blood sugar levels, depresses the immune system, and damages arteries and the heart, contributing to heart disease.[6]

HEALTHY ANGER HAS TREMENDOUS POTENTIAL FOR GOOD

We need to continually remind ourselves that anger is energy, and energy is neutral. While we have minimal control over the fact that we *experience* anger, we can have total control over how we choose to *express* that anger. We can choose to harness and channel anger-energy in healthy, positive, and constructive ways; we can choose to spend it by expressing it in the same old unhealthy ways, *or* we can choose to invest it in building a healthier relationship.

As you understand God's purpose in giving us the emotion of anger and as you become more aware of the many constructive and positive functions of anger, you will be able to see for yourself why some couples consider anger one of their most valuable emotions. Steve and Jane, the newlywed couple we talked about at the beginning of the chapter, learned creative ways to invest their anger-energy, developed more effective anger management skills, and realized that healthy anger really can be an invaluable tool in cultivating an intimate marriage. They discovered that anger is really a signal.

Anger Is a Signal

One of anger's most valuable services is that it can serve as an alarm or warning sign that we need to take a look at some aspect of our lives or relationships. It can make us aware of issues that need our attention. It may be that we are in danger. Anger can increase our awareness of inequity and injustice. It may help us identify a difference that needs to be addressed.

In. *The Dance of Anger,* Harriet Lerner notes:

> Anger is a signal and one worth listening to. Our anger may be a message that we are being hurt, that our rights are being violated, that our needs or wants are not being adequately met, or simply that something isn't right. Our anger may tell us that we are not addressing an important emotional issue in our lives, or that too much of our self—our beliefs, values, desires or ambitions—is being compromised in a relationship. Our anger may be a signal that we are doing more and giving more than we can comfortably do or give. Or our anger may warn us that others are doing too much for us, at the expense of our own competence and growth. Just as physical pain tells us to take our hand off the hot stove, the pain of our anger preserves the very integrity of our self. Our anger can motivate us to say no to the ways in which we are defined by others and yes to the dictates of our inner self.[7]

The anger that both Steve and Jane were experiencing was a warning signal that there were some relational issues they needed to address. Anger is an emotion that God can use to get our attention and make us more aware of opportunities to learn, to grow, to deepen, to mature, and to make significant changes for the good.

Anger is to our lives like a smoke detector is to a house, like a dash warning light is to a car, and like a flashing yellow light is to a driver. Each of those serve as a kind of warning or alarm to stop, look, and listen. They say, "Take caution, something might be wrong."

Anger Is a Powerful Source of Motivation

Lee Iacocca provides us with a powerful example of the constructive motivational potential of anger. In 1979, *The Wall Street Journal* published a devastating editorial criticizing Chrysler's mismanagement, concluding that the nearly bankrupt company should be allowed to "die with dignity." When he read the editorial, Iacocca got mad, but he realized he was faced with three choices: He could lash out in anger at the *Journal* and condemn and criticize them and thus do more damage to himself, he could ignore the criticism and hope it would go away, or he could invest the energy of his anger and use the criticism to motivate his people. In an excerpt from one of his speeches, Iacocca tells his response:

> I got mad. . . . My colleagues in Highland Park got mad. Tens of thousands of Chrysler people all across America got mad. Our labor unions, our suppliers, and our lenders all got mad. We got so mad, we banded together, we talked things over, and working together, we fixed what was wrong at Chrysler.
>
> We doubled our productivity. We rejuvenated our factories. We cut our costs. We started building the highest quality cars and trucks made in America. In short, we turned things around. Now, we're selling cars and making lots of money. . . . This story has a moral. Wonderful things can happen when Americans get mad. I think some well-directed anger can cure most of what's wrong in America today.[8]

Anger Provides the Power to Protect Those You Love

Several years ago there was a story in the news about an eighty-five-year-old man who with his wife and her sister were visiting New York City. They had just finished seeing a play and were getting into their car to leave. His wife and her sister got in the front seat and he got in the backseat.

As his wife started the car, two young men, one of them with a pistol in his hand, came up to the car, opened the door, and demanded that the women give them their jewelry and purses. At first they didn't see the old man sitting in the backseat. As they turned to take off with the loot, they noticed the man. As one of the men started to open the back door, the elderly man turned toward it, placed his feet against it, and pushed as hard as he could. The robber was caught by surprise, and the force of the door knocked him off balance. His gun flew from his hand, and as he recovered from his surprise he and his accomplice fled, leaving the loot behind them.

One of the first questions the media asked the elderly man was, "Why did you do it?" His immediate response was, "I don't know. If I'd had time to think about it I probably wouldn't have done it." He said that he was first aware of feeling fear, but when he heard the fear in the quivering voices of his wife and sister-in-law, he found himself getting angry. *In what seemed to him like an automatic response, his anger gave him the power and strength to protect those he loved and to protect himself.*

When we harness the power of anger it can be a source of strength and provide protection. It can keep us from being a victim. It can help us break free from the immobilization of worry and fear and empower us for constructive action.

Healthy Anger Can Lead Us to More Intimate Relationships

What? You've got to be kidding me! Anger can help us become more intimate? That's right! But notice we said *healthy* anger.

Over the past twenty years we've found that there are several characteristics of couples who have learned how to make their anger work *for* them. They develop more effective communication skills, are more creative, are better at problem-solving, find it easier to trust each other, and experience much deeper levels of intimacy and security.

Disagreements may involve the emotions of fear, hurt, and frustration. Jane expressed fear that their relationship was threatened and that she would never be understood. Steve expressed hurt over what had been said to him and how it had been said. They both expressed frustration that they'd had similar disagreements before and this felt like the same song, twenty-seventh verse. Disagreements often involve anger and lead to conflict.

At this point in the process, Steve and Jane had a choice, and you have a choice too. We can choose to spend our anger-energy by dumping on our spouse or child and show them where, once again, they are clearly wrong and where we, as usual, are right. Or we can throw up our hands in futility and stomp out of the room. By that act we communicate one of two things: Either the other person is not worth taking the time to work out the issue with or communication between the two of us is impossible. Both choices lead to feelings of hopelessness and helplessness and set us up for more failure in the future.

However, there is another option. We can acknowledge our fear, hurt, or frustration and choose to invest our anger-energy by seizing this opportunity to better understand our loved one. One of the most practical ways to "bear all things, believe all things, hope all things, and endure all things" (1 Corinthians 13) is to develop the habit of working through our differences. This takes time and involves listening, asking questions, listening again, asking more questions, and finally reaching understanding.

Steve and Jane are a great example of how little differences can push the buttons that lead to expressions of anger and over time escalate into major issues. Walls can be built with one little brick of disagreement at a time. That's what had happened to them.

When they came for counseling they thought they had a MAJOR problem and that they were abnormal. They were relieved to discover that what they were experiencing was actually very normal. They began to see their anger as a normal part of a healthy relationship. When they understood that their anger often pointed to a relational difference that could be a window into each other's hearts and a potential pathway to greater intimacy, they became very open to the next steps.

In the next several chapters we're going to teach you what we taught Steve and Jane. You are going to learn practical ways to make your anger work for you and to manage conflict in ways that will actually lead to understanding, an increased sense of safety, greater trust, and deeper levels of intimacy.

When you know someone loves you enough to take the time to work through a difference rather than take a walk out the door, you know that person's love is not a shallow, superficial, conditional love. You know that no matter what happens they aren't going to desert you. You know that you are loved and valued for who you are. You know that you can be secure in his or her love for you. As we will see in later chapters, an increase in security leads to an increase in trust, which creates the perfect environment for deep levels of intimacy to grow.

Our differences and disagreements provide a window of opportunity to better understand and thus appreciate the uniqueness of our spouse. They don't have to escalate to a quarrel, a fight, violence, and abuse. Anger can give us the energy to stay focused, stick with the issue, and bring it to a positive conclusion.

SMALL BEGINNINGS

1. Before you read this book, did you think anger was a negative or a positive emotion?

2. Based on what you've read thus far, in the space below write out your own one-sentence definition of anger:

3. What might be three potentially positive aspects of healthy anger for your marriage relationship?

4. Since anger is a secondary emotion, take advantage of your next experience of anger to begin to develop skills in identifying your primary emotions that may have activated the anger. One of the easiest ways to do this is for you to start keeping an anger log. For the next thirty days keep the anger log handy. Whenever you become aware of any form of anger (remember its various disguises) grab your anger log and fill it out.

Anger Log

Date: _____ Time: _____ Location: _____

Describe the issue:

_____

Intensity: 1 2 3 4 5 6 7 8 9 10

Note: Rate the intensity of your anger on a scale from 1–10. One means it is barely noticeable. Ten means you have gone way beyond anger into an out-of-control rage. If it's a 5 or above continue on through the next steps listed. If it's a 1–4 just make a mental note of it, let go of it, and continue on through your day.

Describe what set you up for or what might have made you more vulnerable to an anger response:

_____

What were some of the warning signs and physiological responses indicating that you might be getting angry?

_____

Primary emotion:

(a) Hurt (b) Frustration (c) Fear (d) Other _____

My self-talk about this situation:

_____

Once a week take twenty to thirty minutes to review your anger log. Ask yourself these questions:

1. Do you see any patterns?
2. Are there certain times of the day, the week, or the month that you are more likely to experience anger?
3. Are there certain primary emotions that more consistently lead to an anger response than others?

4. Are there certain people with whom you are more likely to experience anger?
5. Do you have a stronger or more intense response to some issues than others?
6. What is your self-talk about the issue?

In our own marriage and in over twenty years of work with thousands of other couples, we made an amazing discovery. The majority of people who kept an anger log experienced a noticeable decrease in the unhealthy expressions of their anger. That's right. The simple activity of keeping an anger log and taking a few minutes to review it once a week can be a huge step in the direction of making your anger work for you and having greater intimacy in your marriage relationship. Why not give it a try?

CHAPTER
6

THE MYTHS
OF ANGER

David Augustus Burke's last words were tainted by vengeance: "Hi, Ray. I think it's sort of ironical that we end up like this," he scribbled on an air sickness bag. "I asked for some leniency for my family, remember? Well, I got none, and you'll get none."

No one knows what Ray Thomson told David Burke when he fired him in 1987 for allegedly pocketing $69 in in-flight cocktail receipts. Whatever Thomson said, Burke didn't buy it. Unemployed, spurned by his girlfriend, he apparently began making quiet but methodical preparations for a bizarre murder-suicide mission that would kill a planeload of people. All of the rejection, all of the suppressed and hidden anger exploded 22,000 feet over central California. Shots splintered the calm of a routine commuter flight, and if his calculated death plan of revenge succeeded, at least one shot tore into Thomson.

The pilot radioed, "I have an emergency . . . gunfire." Sounds of a tremendous scuffle would be heard later on a cockpit voice recorder tape. A groan. A gasp. Then PSA flight 1771 plunged nose-first into a cattle ranch in San Luis Obispo County.

A few days later, David's father, Altamont Burke, tried to make sense of the dichotomy. "My son was a gentle guy, but don't talk any trash to him," he said.

Burke, Thomson, and forty-one other persons died. Lying in the rubble was the .44 caliber Magnum that Burke had borrowed from a friend with six cartridges spent. Also found in the horrid carnage was the air sickness bag that spelled out the apparent motive for mass murder.[1]

From many of the newspaper reports and interviews with family and friends it was clear that David Augustus Burke did not appear to be the typical angry person. You might be asking yourself what we mean by a "typical angry person." That's an important question! But let's turn it around. How would *you* describe the typical angry person? When you think of anger or angry people, what comes to mind? Who do you think of first? Perhaps your father or mother, a brother or sister, a husband or wife, a good friend, or . . . yourself. Do you think of someone who is frequently and visibly angry?

That last sentence contains one of the key words many people use to identify an angry person: *visibly*. One of the many myths regarding anger is that if a person doesn't appear on the outside to be angry, then they don't have a problem with anger.

Anger is a complex emotion. It can disguise itself in many ways. One of the major reasons why the emotion of anger has gained a primarily negative reputation is that there is so much misinformation about what anger is and can be. It is truly unfortunate that the mostly incorrect and inaccurate misinformation far outweighs the true and accurate facts regarding this powerful and potentially positive emotion. We've already touched on some of these misconceptions, but let's explore further what we've learned about anger.

Many of these misunderstandings have been sanctioned by our society and have become myths . . . fiction that has become accepted as fact. Read through the following list of Anger Myths. If at any time in your life you have either outwardly agreed with any of these statements or have by your actions functioned as if one or more were true, place a check in the Agree column. For those statements that you have never believed to be true, place a check in the Disagree column. Remember that your response does not necessarily indicate your current belief but rather those statements that you have at some time in your life accepted.[2]

ANGER MYTHS

	Agree	Disagree
1. Since God is love and anger is the opposite of love, it is clear that God is against anger and that whenever we get angry we are sinning.	☐	☐
2. If you don't look or sound angry, you don't have an anger problem.	☐	☐
3. Anger always leads to some form of violence and therefore it is never good to be angry.	☐	☐
4. If I express anger to someone I love it will destroy our relationship. Anger and love just don't mix.	☐	☐
5. Spiritual people don't get angry.	☐	☐
6. The best way to deal with anger is to ignore it. If you ignore anger it will go away.	☐	☐
7. The best way to deal with anger is to stuff it. Expressing anger breeds even more anger and leads to loss of control.	☐	☐
8. The best way to deal with anger is to dump it. Just get all of that anger out of your system. You and everyone else will be better for it.	☐	☐

Since even one of these myths can have a negative impact on building understanding and intimacy in a marriage relationship, it will be valuable for us to explore each one of them:

MYTH #1:
Since God is love and anger is the opposite of love, it is clear that God is against anger and that whenever we get angry we are sinning.

This particular myth, or variations of it, is clearly one of the most common misconceptions about anger.

The Old Testament reports numerous instances in which God expresses anger or is described as being angry. God is described as being angry with the people of Israel for their rebellion—not that His ego was bruised because man wouldn't be subject to Him; on the contrary, His anger had its source in His love. It resulted in discipline and acts of love designed to restore a broken relationship with Him. God's anger revealed how much God cared. It revealed His patience and His love. So God's anger arises, in part, out of love for us.

In contrast, with men and women anger often arises out of bitterness and hatred. In fact, the association is so strong in some of our minds that the two are often seen as synonymous. Anger becomes a sign of hatred. This error can make it difficult to understand God's anger. Some of us have never clearly seen the distinction between anger and hate. Thus, we may believe that God is primarily a punitive God who acts out of His hate for certain people. This thinking implies a very small and insecure God—one who gets upset at every offense to His pride, a God who turns quickly from love to hate, depending on His mood at the moment.

This confusion of anger with hate can only be corrected by a careful study of truth in Scripture. Psalm 106:40 declares, "The Lord was angry with his people." It is clear that the rebellion of His people caused the anger, but further reading shows that this is not the emotion of hate. The response is not of punishment but of discipline and correction. Yes, He did hand them over to their enemies. But then: "Many times he delivered them. . . . He took note of their distress. . . .

He remembered his covenant and out of his great love he relented" (vv. 43–45).

These aren't acts of hate. Here we see God's anger arise out of love. It is a means whereby God communicates His character. It is intended to convey that discipline has its foundations in love. Anger brings reality to the seriousness of the relationship.

In the middle of writing this chapter I (Gary) received a phone call from a friend who, for years, has been struggling with being a workaholic and with taking on too many projects. He has used his busyness as a way to run from and avoid dealing with both personal and relationship issues, especially problems in his marriage. When he told me about his schedule for the next several months I told him that I was angry with him. My anger was not caused by hatred for him . . . just the opposite. My anger arose because of my love for him and my deep concern for his health and well-being.

In a marriage relationship, if we're not able to make a clear distinction between anger and hate, it will be difficult for our hearts to be truly free to love. Love will express itself at times as anger. If anger is interpreted by our spouse as hate, the love itself is questioned since to him or her all anger arises from hate. As legitimate love is misinterpreted it can be rejected, damaging the relationship with the potential for the rejected love to turn into bitterness and hatred.

Paul destroys the myth that all anger is sin when he says, "Be angry, and yet do not sin; do not let the sun go down on your anger, and do not give the devil an opportunity" (Ephesians 4:26–27 NASB). Paul makes it very clear that while it is normal to experience anger, we can choose to express that anger in ways that are not sinful.

This distinction between the *experience* of anger and the *expression* of anger is a significant one. In fact, one of the most basic errors of many of the anger myths that plague so many people is a failure to make this distinction.

On one hand, the experience of anger is a normal and natural one. A part of what is involved in being made in God's image is that we have emotions, and one of those emotions is anger. We can allow our anger to dominate and control us or we can, with God's help and a little bit of work on our part, learn how to make the emotion of anger work for us rather than against us.

For each one of these Anger Myths a few corrections can be made so that what was an Anger Myth can be turned into an Anger Fact.

Anger Fact #1: God is love, and one expression of God's love for us is that He created us in His image. Since God has emotions, we have emotions, including anger. Our anger, like God's, can be motivated by love. Getting angry is not a sin. We can choose our expression of anger. God is glorified and we are healthier and happier when we choose to express the emotion of anger in healthy and constructive ways.

MYTH #2:
If you don't look or sound angry, you don't have an anger problem.

This myth assumes that whenever we experience the emotion of anger we are probably aware of it, and it can't help but reveal itself in some way. Some individuals do have a difficult time hiding what they feel. Even a stranger can look at their face or listen to their voice and tell what is going on inside of them. But there are a lot of people for whom this is not the case; they are pretty good at hiding their emotions.

Ed was among those. He appeared to be the perfect pastor: always pleasant, always agreeable, and always available. He avoided conflict like the plague, under the guise of being a peacemaker.

During Ed and Amy's courtship Ed appeared to be the perfect guy. He seemed to enjoy Amy's friends and was loving and thoughtful with Amy's parents. However, it didn't take long into the marriage for a different side to emerge. He began to be increasingly negative and critical of many of Amy's habits, her friends, and even her parents.

In the first counseling session Ed began to unload his emotional dump truck of hurts, wounds, and frustrations. Amy stared at him in disbelief. "I had absolutely no idea that these things bothered you," she said in an astonished tone of voice. "In fact, some of the things you are saying frustrate you about my friends and family are things you told me you liked about them."

Ed is like many people who at times are angry but aren't aware of it, or if they are, have for a variety of reasons learned to repress, suppress, deny, or ignore it. At the beginning of this chapter we shared the story of David Burke. His friends described him as kind and gentle, someone who was anything but the stereotypical angry man. But he had a major anger problem. His inability or unwillingness to deal with his anger in constructive ways led to the destruction of himself and forty-two innocent people.

Anger Fact #2: Just because you don't look or feel angry, or because your friends wouldn't describe you as an angry person, doesn't mean you don't have a problem with anger. Anyone who does not understand and appreciate the potential value of anger may have a problem with anger. Anyone who hasn't developed healthy ways to express their anger has a problem with anger.

MYTH #3:
Anger always leads to some form of violence, and therefore it is never good to be angry.

This third anger myth is an especially interesting one. The vast majority of people who have responded to our questionnaire on anger myths have indicated that they have never believed or accepted this particular myth. However, in sitting down with couples and discussing their ways of dealing with anger, things change. One spouse will make the observation that while his or her partner may not consciously agree with this myth, he or she behaves as if it were true.

Cathy is a good example of this situation. Cathy and her husband,

Tim, have raised five children. Cathy and Tim first came in for help with conflict resolution. They had struggled for many years trying to solve both marital and parenting kinds of problems. Most of the time they settled on a short-term compromise but were never able to identify or deal with the core issues.

Cathy was proud to be able to state that she was not an angry person and that, as far as she knew, she rarely even experienced the emotion of anger. Yet she did admit that she was frequently forgetful, tended to avoid problems, was often late, liked to change the subject, and had some good skills in the use of subtle sarcasm.

Cathy indicated that her father had been an alcoholic. She was quick to add that she didn't think that she had been affected by his alcoholism. As we discussed her family in greater detail, Cathy began to talk about what it was like being the oldest child in a dysfunctional family. She would wait up for her father on weekend nights: "I would keep my bedroom window open and listen for how he would drive the car into the driveway, how he would slam the car door, the sound of his walking up the steps . . . then, of course, I would listen for the tone of his voice. Certain signs always told me whether or not he would be beating Mom that night. I always knew when I had to gather the kids up and get them out of the way." She went on to add that "whenever Dad got angry, he would beat either Mom or one of the kids."

At an early age, Cathy had learned to equate anger and violence. To her, the experience of anger and its expression through violence had become synonymous. Since she had vowed to herself that she would never be like her father, she simply denied any feelings of anger with the idea that if she was never angry she would never be violent.

Over a period of several months, Cathy and Tim learned to distinguish between the experience of anger and the various ways in which anger can be expressed. Cathy learned that while she had frequently experienced the emotion of anger, she had simply found different ways to express it. While her passive and indirect expressions of anger were not as violent as her father's active and direct expressions, both ways of dealing with anger were unhealthy.

Cathy's denial of anger served to obscure and hide her true hurts, needs, and concerns from Tim and even from herself. Therefore, both of them were frustrated and unfulfilled, and had at best a superficial relationship. As Cathy and Tim learned how to better understand and deal with the emotion of anger, they were then free to identify and deal with core issues in their marriage, and thus experience the deep intimacy that each was seeking.

It is obvious that Anger Myth #3 is just that . . . a myth. How could you reword and correct Anger Myth #3 and turn it into an Anger Fact? Write your response in the space below:

Anger Fact #3:[3]

_____

_____

MYTH #4:
If I express anger to someone I love it will destroy our relationship. Anger and love just don't mix.

Brian and Michelle's marriage had begun like most marriages. They both had many hopes, dreams, and expectations. During their courtship they talked for hours on end and almost never disagreed. Even on the rare occasions when they did disagree it was never difficult or painful. They took the time to honestly share their ideas, and as a result of the discussion went away from the disagreement with a stronger sense of understanding and oneness.

Within the first six months of marriage it became clear that Brian was much more of an introvert than Michelle. When he came home from work he wanted to be alone for a while to rest and relax, to get his mind off the day's work and to recharge his batteries. Michelle was much more of an extrovert. When she came home from work she wanted to share the events of the day, to talk about what she had done and who she had seen, and then plan some activity for the evening, preferably with friends.

With each passing month their differences became more obvious. They became increasingly frustrated with each other, and as their frustration increased, so did their anger. Both Brian and Michelle had been raised in good Christian homes. They both believed that it was wrong to get angry and that expressing anger could jeopardize their marriage. To them, any expression of anger was negative, unspiritual, and immature.

So what did they do? Brian dealt with his anger by hiding. He continued to retreat more and more into his computer and into his love of watching sports on television. Michelle dealt with her anger in an opposite but equally ineffective way. She took on extra jobs at work. She became more active at church by joining the choir and teaching a third-grade Sunday school class. They both felt misunderstood, unaccepted, unloved, and very alone.

What was the result of not identifying and constructively expressing and dealing with their anger? It was destroying their relationship. They were becoming married singles.

It is vital for us to understand that while anger and love are separate emotions, the greater our love for someone the greater the potential for frustration, hurt, and anger. By not being in touch with and communicating the root sources of their anger to each other, Brian and Michelle were not allowing each other to understand their hurts and frustrations. By not sharing their hurts and frustrations, they were robbing themselves of the opportunity to better understand each other, more effectively love each other, and enjoy the depths of intimacy they both longed for.

Anger Fact #4: If I am aware of my experience of anger and choose to express it to someone I love in healthy ways, it can be used of God to increase our mutual understanding and help strengthen and enrich our relationship.

MYTH #5:
Spiritual people don't get angry.

Spiritual people love. Spiritual people are compassionate. Spiritual people are concerned. Spiritual people can be discouraged. Spiritual people experience hurt, frustration, and fear. Spiritual people experience anger.

No human being is immune from experiencing the full range of human emotions. One of the occupational hazards of being human is that we will experience the full range of emotions, including the very basic human emotion of anger. From the nursery to the nursing home the emotion of anger is a universal experience.

Experiencing the emotion of anger has nothing to do with being naughty or nice, unspiritual or spiritual, immature or mature. But when we talk about how we choose to express the emotion of anger . . . that's a different story. We can choose to express our anger in ways that help or in ways that hinder, in ways that build up or in ways that destroy. We can be irresponsible and allow the emotion of anger to control us and express that anger in cruel and violent ways. We can also be wise and not let the emotion of anger control us but choose to express that anger in healthy and positive ways. That's what this book is all about.

Anger Fact #5: Anger is a fact of life. Everyone experiences anger. Smart people choose to understand their experience of anger. Healthy people choose to express anger in constructive ways.

MYTH #6:
The best way to deal with anger is to ignore it. If you ignore anger it will go away.

Imagine that you are driving down the street and you notice that the red warning light has come on. You are running a bit late and don't have the time to check the source of the problem. You decide to simply ignore it. After all, if it just came on it can't be that serious. After driving a few more miles the red light begins to bother you. You reach across the seat into your briefcase and pull out a small yellow Post-it note and place it over the red warning light. Now that you can't see the warning light you feel much better.

Does ignoring the red warning light make good sense? Will it help your car run better or get to its destination faster? *Of course not!* It's interesting that what many of us would never think of doing with our automobiles we do on a daily basis with our emotions and thus with our bodies.

As we said in chapter 5, one of the many potentially positive aspects of anger is that it can serve as a very powerful and effective warning system. Healthy anger can help us identify problems and needs and provide us with the energy to do something about them.

This anger myth really has two parts and both are erroneous. The first part suggests that ignoring anger can be healthy. The second part suggests that anger and the issues that led to it will somehow magically disappear. To say that ignoring our anger is healthy makes about as much sense as saying that it is healthy to ignore chest pain. Ignoring anger can be hazardous to your health.

On a short-term basis it may seem like ignoring our anger is a wise choice. Just like our imaginary driver, we cover up the red warning light. There are usually few, if any, immediate consequences. At the moment the light was covered, the car didn't stop. In fact, not only did the car keep on running, but there was no longer any irritating red warning light to contend with. Unfortunately, in most cases the car would not run very long. And when it did break down the repair bill would invariably be much more expensive than if the driver had heeded the warning.

When we ignore the hurts, frustrations, and fears that lead to our anger, they don't just go away. In fact, they tend to get worse and become an even greater problem for us to deal with in the future.

Over the years we've discovered that whenever we ignore or bury an emotion it is buried alive. At some time and in some way that ignored or buried emotion will express itself—physically, psychologically, or spiritually. This principle is especially true as it relates to the powerful emotion of anger. What are some of the long-term costs of ignoring our anger?

There is a growing body of research that strongly suggests that ignoring anger has detrimental effects on your health. A twelve-year longitudinal study of ten thousand people revealed that those who suppressed anger were more than twice as likely to die of heart disease as those who expressed anger in healthy ways. A twenty-five-year study showed that people with high hostility scores had higher incidence of heart disease; they were also six times more likely to die by age fifty from all causes of disease than their low-scoring counterparts. Other research over a twenty-year period correlated higher hostility scores with increased rates of not only coronary heart disease but also cancer, accidents, and suicide.[4]

Anger Fact #6: Anger is one of the most powerful of all the God-given emotions, and ignoring your experience of anger is almost invariably hazardous to your emotional, psychological, physical, and spiritual health. Ignoring anger is an unhealthy choice. In the short run it hinders us from dealing with the real issues, and in the long run it significantly increases the probability of developing real physical problems. When we do experience the emotion of anger, there are a variety of healthy ways in which this emotion can be expressed—ignoring it is far from the only option.

MYTH #7:
The best way to deal with anger is to stuff it. Expressing anger breeds even more anger and leads to loss of control.

Stuffing anger? Isn't that the same thing as ignoring anger? What's the difference?

When you ignore your anger you don't acknowledge it and you may not even be aware of it. If (heaven forbid) you are aware of it you pretend it isn't important and doesn't really exist.

When you stuff your anger you are very much aware of it, but you consciously choose to sit on it, to keep it in, to hold it down, and you hope that nobody notices. For whatever reason—fear of offending someone, fear of losing control, fear of looking bad—stuffing it and looking good appear to be the healthiest option.

In his book *Free for the Taking*, missionary Joseph Cooke tells how he tried to suppress his anger:

> Squelching our feelings never pays. In fact, it's rather like plugging up a steam vent in a boiler. When the steam is stopped in one place, it will come out somewhere else. Either that or the whole business will blow up in your face. And bottled-up feelings are just the same. If you bite down your anger, for example, it often comes out in another form that is more difficult to deal with. It changes into sullenness, self-pity, depression, or snide, cutting remarks. . . .
>
> Not only may bottled-up emotions come out sideways in various unpleasant forms; they also may build up pressure until they simply have to burst, and when they do, someone is almost always bound to get hurt.
>
> I remember that for years of my life, I worked to bring my emotions under control. Over and over again, as they cropped up, I would master them in my attempt to achieve what looked like a

gracious . . . Christian spirit. Eventually I had nearly everybody fooled, even in a measure my own wife. But it was all a fake. I had a nice-looking outward appearance, but inside the mass of feelings lay bottled up. But they were there nevertheless. And the time came when the whole works blew up in my face, in an emotional breakdown.

All the things that had been stuffed for so long came out in the open. Frankly, there was no healing, no recovery, no building a new life for me until all those feelings were sorted out, and until I learned to know them for what they were, accept them, and find some way of expressing them honestly and nondestructively.[5]

Anger Fact #7 (similar to Anger Fact #6): When in doubt about what to do with your experience of anger, don't stuff it. Choose a healthy way to express your anger. Unhealthy expressions of anger breed even more anger. They can be destructive and lead to loss of control. Healthy expressions of anger allow you to deal with the root issues and decrease anger. They are constructive and lead to greater control.

MYTH #8:
The best way to deal with anger is to dump it. Just get all of that anger out of your system. You and everyone else will be better for it.

This popular myth sounds good and, on the surface, seems to make sense. Unfortunately, it is not true. A classic example of someone who seems to have believed and practiced this myth is late football coach Woody Hayes. The following article appeared in *Time* magazine in 1979:

Coach Wayne Woodrow Hayes, sixty-five, the autocrat of Ohio State football for twenty-eight years, was fired after assaulting an opposing player. . . . Violent outbursts were a hallmark of his coaching career. "Woody's idea of sublimating," an acquaintance once said, "is to hit someone." . . . The people closest to him never seemed to lose patience. . . . Yet he was always frighteningly—even pathologically—at the mercy of private demons. "When we lose a game, nobody's madder at me than me," he said five years ago. "When I look into the mirror in the morning, I want to take a swing at me." Literally. After losing to Iowa in 1963, Hayes slashed his face with a large ring on his left hand. Pacing the sidelines, he sometimes bit into the fleshy heel of his hand until it bled. Even a heart attack in 1974 did not make Hayes ease up.[6]

What a tragic legacy! Today when many people think of Coach Woody Hayes they think of a man who was a success at coaching college football but who was a failure at understanding and dealing with his emotions. It is possible for some people to be successful at what they do, at least for a while, and to be a failure in who they are. For a while Hayes was able to get by with his unhealthy ways of expressing his anger, but eventually it caught up with him. He was fired from the job he so dearly loved. He was disgraced. His legacy was tarnished.

Both practical experience and recent research suggests that simply talking about our anger and/or dumping it does not reduce it. In fact, just the opposite takes place . . . it rehearses and enlarges it. We've learned that in the vast majority of cases, ventilation or dumping of anger does not in any way act as a catharsis. On the contrary, individuals became more hostile rather than less hostile as a result of dumping their anger.

Carol Tavris has done an extensive review of research on anger. She reports that in study after study the results indicate that not only does dumping not decrease anger but it can freeze a hostile disposition. One psychologist who initially held the assumption that people who repress anger are in worse mental health than those who express anger was Mary K. Biaggios. She gave 150 college students a battery of tests to prove her point. The results surprised her. She found that the students who were quick to express anger were less self-controlled, less tolerant, and more inflexible than students who took the time to process what they were feeling and choose an appropriate response.[7]

Anger Fact #8: When you are angry and you are in doubt about what you want to do, don't dump it. Take time to understand your experience of anger and you will be better able to choose a healthy and constructive way to express it.

Most couples we work with are surprised at the degree to which they have believed many of the anger myths and the degree to which those myths have negatively impacted their marriage relationship. If you are at all like the many couples we've worked with, we're sure you've had a lot of "ahas" as you've read through this chapter.

Once we sat down and looked at our marriage, we were amazed at how our own anger myths had built walls of fear, indifference, distance, and shame. For example, I (Gary) grew up with the idea that anger was always bad, always negative, and always a sin. I believed *Myth #5: Spiritual people don't get angry.* I thought that a godly man and a spiritual leader didn't really struggle with anger. So whenever I felt anything close to anger, I did all I could to hide it. But as we've seen in this chapter, you can't hide it indefinitely.

In addition to accepting many of the anger myths as facts, we didn't grow up with models of what healthy expressions of anger looked like. Passionate people that we were (and by God's grace still are), we both struggled with anger but expressed it in two significantly different ways, neither of which was healthy or helpful. We discovered that only after we were able to identify and begin to eliminate some of our own anger myths were we in a place to take the next step on the pathway to a truly intimate marriage—learning how to express anger in ways that tore down walls of fear, hurt, and pain and built bridges of understanding, trust, and intimacy.

SMALL BEGINNINGS

An important first step in developing healthier ways of responding to anger is to identify and become more aware of our existing unhealthy patterns.

Take just a few minutes to review the list of anger myths found at the beginning of this chapter. From this list of eight anger myths pick the three that have been most influential in your life. Using 3x5 cards, write each unhealthy anger myth on one side and the healthy anger fact on the other side.

Carry these cards with you, and for the next thirty days look at them several times a day. You might be surprised at how powerful this simple exercise can be.

THE MANY FACES
OF ANGER

Rick and Jennifer had been married for twelve years and had four precious children. They both expressed a deep love for each other and a strong commitment to their marriage. They called for counseling to work on some communication problems, but it didn't take long for one of their core concerns to emerge.

It was in the middle of our first session that Rick finally opened up. "For many years I've struggled with my anger. It seems like I can go along for a while and it's not a problem and then all of a sudden some small thing will happen. I lose my temper and usually say something I'm sorry for later." Glancing at Jennifer he continued, "I'm not the only one in my family with an anger problem. My father, who is a wonderful Christian man, has for many years had a reputation for being hot-headed. He doesn't get angry very often, but when he does, watch out."

With a note of sadness in his voice Rick continued, "I didn't realize it was as bad as it is until Jennifer and I got married." He then began to relate an all-too-common story of little hurts and frustrations building into painful expressions of unhealthy anger that wounded the people he loved most. In Rick's case it would usually start out as negative and critical comments that led to a biting sarcasm that at times would result in a verbal explosion.

We explained to Rick and Jennifer what most couples are surprised to learn: Marriage probably generates more anger than they will experience in any other relationship. When two people live together with a commitment to increasing closeness, vulnerability, and intimacy, the potential for fear, hurt, frustration, and misunderstanding is enormous—which means there is also great potential for anger.

After a deep and thoughtful sigh Rick slumped down in his seat and asked, "Is there any way I can get rid of my anger?" Our response caught him by surprise. "Rick, the problem isn't the emotion of anger. The problem is that you don't understand the difference between healthy and unhealthy anger, and you haven't learned how to express your anger in healthy ways." He immediately responded, "Healthy anger . . . you've got to be kidding me!" He continued, "I've heard anger referred to in many ways, but never in the context of being healthy." If you are like Rick, and most people that we've worked with, you would have had the same response.

By now you've learned that anger is a God-given emotion that can be expressed in healthy and unhealthy ways. Through your anger log you've learned what's unique about your experience of anger. In the last chapter you became aware of some of your own anger myths that have kept you stuck in the rut of unhealthy anger and kept you from making your anger work for you. At this point you may be asking, "How do I begin to change my automatic and unconscious ways of responding? Where do I start?"

Sometimes our emotional patterns are so automatic they are hard to identify. As children we all experienced events that elicited anger. What might have started out as a conscious reaction became an unconscious reaction over time and with many repetitions. Because it is so automatic it seems like it's a part of who we are rather than a style that has been learned, and thus a style that with God's help can be changed.

The first and easiest step in the growth process is to identify your characteristic style of experiencing and expressing anger. Throughout the book we've seen that anger can come packaged in many different shapes and sizes. It hides behind many different masks. Over our lifetime each one of us has developed our own unique reaction pattern or style of dealing with anger. However, when it comes to expressing anger, most of us tend to fall into one of three unhealthy reactive styles.[1]

PASSIVE REACTORS—THE CREAM PUFF

"Cream puffs" are nice people who are characteristically passive and avoid any direct expression of anger. In situations that for most people would evoke some expression of anger and protest, they will often remain silent. They avoid making clear statements about what they think and feel, especially when their opinions might make someone else uncomfortable. They are more likely to say "I'm sorry" than "I'm hurt," "I'm afraid," "I'm frustrated," or "I'm angry."

Since cream puffs often fail to share their own legitimate needs and concerns, those who are closest to them may be unaware of their pain. Most of their energy is focused on protecting others, maintaining harmonious relationships, and keeping the peace. Over time they become less and less aware of their own needs. They can even become so focused on hearing what everyone else has to say that they fail to hear what the Lord has to say. God's truths become real to everyone else but them.

Another feature of cream puffs is that they avoid conflict like the plague. Many of us grew up with an unconscious and powerful fear of conflict, but for cream puffs even the possibility of conflict can produce tremendous anxiety. Anything that might be construed as arguing or fighting can feel potentially dangerous and wrong.

Over time this inability to address deep problems and the desire to avoid conflict only make things worse. As it gets worse they experience even more fear, hurt, frustration, and anger, and as those feelings smolder they lead to a deep sense of hopelessness, helplessness, and despair. What's the result? The cream puff becomes overwhelmed with discouragement and depression, overrun with guilt and shame, and unable to do anything.

Many cream puffs appear as if they never struggle with anger. Somehow they've been able to shut it off. Unfortunately, our emotions don't work that way. Yes, for a limited time we can choose not to express it, but the emotion is still there. When we think the anger faucet has been turned off, what has really happened is that the hose has merely been bent. Because nothing is coming out, we can begin to think that nothing is there. However, when the pressure becomes great enough the anger will burst out and the cream puff will either implode with health and/or psychological problems or they will explode and spew the hurt and pain on those they love the most.

Jennifer acknowledged that she had grown up as a classic cream puff. Whenever she felt anything close to anger she would either ignore it or think of some way she might be responsible for the problem. She was afraid of conflict and afraid that if she confronted Rick he would explode. One of Jennifer's anger triggers was Rick's tendency to be late, especially for meals. For most of their marriage she made excuses for Rick's being late by telling herself that it was unavoidable or that if she prepared better meals for him to come home to he would be on time. She told herself that someday he would change.

But it didn't work. She continued to experience a growing frustration that turned into anger. It became harder and harder to ignore it. One day when Rick waltzed into the house over forty minutes late, the years of repression, suppression, and denial exploded to the surface. The quiet and passive Jennifer became a volcanic Mt. St. Helens. She decided that Rick wasn't the only one who had an anger problem.

If we don't learn how to express our anger in healthy ways it will eventually express itself, often in ways that are unhealthy and destructive. Why? The answer is simple. As we saw in the last chapter, whenever you bury anger or any other emotion, it is buried alive. Whenever you stuff, suppress, repress, or ignore your anger it will come out, and usually with drastic results. One of the greatest dangers facing cream puffs is that they can only bury their anger for so long. When the emotional dam bursts, the flood can have devastating results.

Deep levels of intimacy are impossible when our ways of relating to others consist of giving in, giving up, and going along; when we assume responsibility for other people's happiness; when we pretend that everything is going great when we know that it isn't; when we are so focused on everyone else that we ignore God's promises, provision, and plan for our own lives.

The typical cream puff is characterized by the following:

anger suppressed	dependent	over-responsible
anger turned inward	doesn't make waves	passive reactor
apathetic	gives in	peace at any price
avoids problems	guilt-prone	self-condemnation
conflict avoider	neglects self	self-pity
denial	over-controlled	toxic shame

AGGRESSIVE REACTORS— THE LOCOMOTIVE

At the opposite extreme are the aggressive reactors or "locomotives." While cream puffs don't give adequate attention to their personal needs, locomotives can be insensitive to the needs of others. They can be so preoccupied with themselves and their own issues that they may not even be aware of the deep needs of those they love the most.

Whereas the anger of cream puffs is usually implosive, the anger of locomotives is most often explosive. When they get angry everyone around them knows it, and anyone within shouting distance is in danger of being yelled at, shamed, and blamed. In fact, one of the fears that keeps many cream puffs locked in their prison of passivity is the fear that if they ever let themselves get in touch with their anger they will become like locomotives.

Here are ten attitudes that, if consistently cultivated, are guaranteed to transform you into the unpopular and offensive person known and disliked as the locomotive:

1. Few people can be trusted. Therefore always be suspicious. Assume the worst about everyone.
2. Material possessions are more important than relationships. Learn to love things and use people.
3. Since you are usually right it isn't necessary to waste much time listening to another person's point of view.
4. Take everything as seriously as possible.
5. There is always enough time to do at least one more thing.
6. Don't forgive and never forget. That's for suckers and fools. Besides that, you'll probably get hurt if you do.
7. Assume that you are always right. It's easier, it feels better, and if you come on strong others will tend to doubt themselves and give in to you.
8. Don't think before speaking. You're probably right the first time.
9. Have no compassion for people who are suffering. The weak deserve what they get.
10. Remember that every silver lining has a cloud. Nothing is ever as good as it seems. If you look hard enough you can always find something to be critical about or worry about.

On the outside locomotives appear confident, but inside they are riddled with fears and insecurities. Frequently they came from homes in which they suffered parental rejection, hostility, and rage. There were no models of healthy anger. What they learned is that aggression can be an effective way to keep people at a distance so others can't hurt them. It can also be a way to pay back those who have hurt them.

Because they need so much acceptance, it is difficult for locomotives to compliment others. Their outbursts give them the attention they believe they deserve and need for themselves. They need to be right all of the time, and when they err it will be on the side of being tough, not tender.

When locomotives get provoked they are likely to label, put down, attack, and humiliate others. They often communicate in ways that trample the dignity and feelings of other people. People who make a habit of dumping their anger on others tend to get angrier more often, not less angry. When we choose to deal with our anger by reacting aggressively it is easy for the anger to become rage. It doesn't take much for locomotives to reach the boiling point and become steaming mad, spewing a verbal shower of acid rain.

At this point it might be helpful to clarify the difference between anger and rage. Mismanaged anger leads to hostility, which leads to a rage that is more powerful, more volatile, and much harder to control. Rage often leads to a desire for revenge that can result in verbal or physical attacks or even murder. When rage runs rampant it can destroy other people, and eventually it will destroy us. John Lee says:

> Rage is the father throwing his infant child against the wall and killing her. Rage is the mother scalding her child with boiling water to teach a lesson. Rage is the husband choking the family dog because it sneaked into the house. Rage is the driver who tailgates you for ten miles blowing his horn because you cut him off by mistake. Rage is the good churchgoer who takes a shotgun and kills five strangers on the street, then blows his own head off. Rage is awful and has no decent place in normal human relationships. Not at home. Not at work. Not in public.[2]

Is there a difference between people who get angry and angry people? Yes! From time to time everyone experiences anger. However, when our expression of anger dominates our lives and becomes a dominant feature of our personality, we have shifted from being a person with anger to an angry person.

Remember that the emotion of anger is one of the most powerful of all the emotions. When we experience anger, a dose of adrenaline and noradrenaline is pumped into our central and peripheral nervous systems. If anger provides one dose of energy, then rage is like taking a triple dose. Over time people can become addicted to the adrenaline rush they get from being enraged and can become rageaholics. According to Proverbs 22:24, this is the type of person we are to avoid at all costs.

Most locomotives believe that venting their hostility and rage helps them achieve their goals. Unfortunately, just the opposite is true. Explosive, out-of-control anger builds walls and blows up bridges. It drains us of energy that could be invested in solving problems. It stimulates negative feelings in ourselves and others and both irritates and alienates those around us.

What are some characteristics of the locomotive?

anger against others	has all the answers	prone to violence
blatant sarcasm	hostile	punitive
combative	loud	quick to blame
critical	obnoxious	rage
cruel teasing	over-competitive	seeks revenge
driven	over-concern for self	shallow
few intimate friends	power hungry	under-responsible

Is there any hope for the locomotive? Susan Jacoby shares an encouraging story that says the answer is yes:

> Looking back on my childhood and early adulthood, it seems to me that I was always apologizing to someone for words spoken in the heat of anger. I exploded at people I loved and those I disliked, at family, friends, strangers, professional peers and even my bosses.
>
> Then, when I was 23, an incident at work literally changed my life. I was attached to a team of investigative reporters (my first real job), and our boss was transferred to another department of the newspaper. We knew that Bob, a man we all liked very much, had been asked to replace him, and we were extremely disappointed when Bob turned down the job. Then an older editor called me into his office and explained that I—and my reputation for responding furiously to any criticism—was the problem.
>
> "Bob told me he just didn't want to put himself in a situation in which every little professional dispute would blow up into a big fight," the editor explained. Then he said something that hurt enormously at the time but turned out to be the biggest favor anyone

has ever done me. "You know," he said, "you're very talented. If you weren't, you would have been fired long ago, because it's so hard to work with you. You can't take criticism without blowing up, even if the criticism is justified. And if the criticism is not justified, you have no idea how to bring other people around to your way of thinking without screaming and insulting them. Your anger is going to do you in if you don't learn how to express it differently."

I was wounded and humiliated and—for once—had nothing to say. I usually forgot my outbursts as soon as they were over, and it was a revelation to learn that other people didn't forget so easily.

This realization was the beginning of a lifelong effort to control my anger—to separate the trivial from the genuinely important and to express truly legitimate anger in ways that were destructive neither to myself nor to others. At age 39, I still haven't succeeded entirely—but I have come a long way.[3]

PASSIVE-AGGRESSIVE REACTORS— THE STEEL MAGNOLIA

When it comes to identifying their unhealthy anger style, the majority of people would put themselves in the cream puff or locomotive category. However, there is a third anger style that in some ways is more subtle and complicated than the first two but just as unhealthy. This third reactive style involves a combination of the first two. As we were working on this chapter Carrie received the following letter:

Dear Mrs. Oliver,

I'm looking forward to your talk at our Women's Fellowship on the subject "Women and Anger."

Could you address the issue of anger in passive-aggressive women? Most of the information I've read or heard about regarding anger deals with the person who shows anger by arguing, throwing things, and being physically abusive, or the person who has inner anger displayed by depression.

The woman whose anger is displayed by hostile looks and subtle gestures that communicate disgust and rejection, or who uses the manipulative power of silence or innuendo to hurt another, is rarely talked about.

Most people perceive this person as quiet, even gentle, because of her passive side. The rage is usually reserved for someone close to her.

I appreciate your taking the time to consider these questions and I hope you'll be able to address them in some way in your talk.

God bless you and your ministry!

Sincerely yours,
Linda

"Steel magnolias" are a confusing contradiction. On the outside they can look like cream puffs—they don't state their needs and are indirect. But if you cross them you'll discover a huge cauldron of bitterness and resentment boiling on the inside. Unhealthy anger is at the core of the passive-aggressive person. Many are good at disguising it, but it's almost impossible to totally conceal.

Cream puffs and locomotives are fairly consistent. Cream puffs can be trusted to yield to the desires and expectations of others in order to gain approval. Locomotives can be trusted to ignore other people's desires and expectations. But steel magnolias are unpredictable. Behind the facade of passivity can lie very aggressive and dangerous motives. Over time they may even convince themselves that they don't have any aggressive feelings. They may act shocked that anyone could misunderstand their pure motives and sincere intentions.

One of the most effective weapons of steel magnolias is sarcasm. Sarcasm involves assault by misdirection, deception, and disguise. It is a way of attacking while avoiding an obviously hostile intent. If anyone responds to what they are really saying, they may be accused of being negative or assuming the worst. Steel magnolias get the message across but don't leave their victims with many options. Proverbs has something to say about this: "A man who is caught lying to his neighbor and says, 'I was just fooling,' is like a madman throwing around firebrands, arrows, and death!" (Proverbs 26:18 TLB).

Steel magnolias are the masters of sending mixed messages and can disguise their anger with a smile and a joke. You know what I mean— the sarcastic, not-so-funny joke that makes people cringe rather than laugh, the one that sounds humorous but carries a sharp yet subtle barb. The anger is disguised as humor and retaliation is discouraged.

And if confronted, they deny being angry. "What's the matter, can't you take a joke?" may be the immediate response. Steel magnolias often make others the butt of their humor and then tell them that they shouldn't be so sensitive or that they need to be a good sport. Their friends and family members end up frustrated, confused, and perhaps even a bit angry themselves.

They key for steel magnolias to start dealing with anger in healthy ways is to recognize that their sarcasm, criticism, negativity, and even chronic lateness are all related to their anger.

What are some characteristics of the steel magnolia?

ambiguity	makes excuses	resentful
carelessness	misunderstanding	silent treatment
chronic lateness	mixed messages	stubbornness
forgetfulness	obstructionism	subtle sarcasm
fosters confusion	procrastination	sulking
inconsistency		

MOVING FROM
REACTING TO RESPONDING

These three reactive anger styles are unhealthy and destructive and significantly minimize the hope for any meaningful intimacy in a marriage. When we stuff, repress, suppress, deny, ignore, or hurl our anger, we are ignoring anger's potentially important message. The reactive styles limit our awareness of the primary emotions that are the real issues and keep us from being able to communicate those concerns to our partner in ways that will help us build bridges of understanding and support.

Reactors deny the painful stuff that's going on inside. Resentment and rage keep them from dealing with legitimate fears and hurts and limit God's ability to bring recovery and restoration. If we don't allow God to help us address the real issues in our lives, how can we ever hope to understand ourselves or our spouses? How can we forgive ourselves or others? And how can we ever grow or achieve any real intimacy?

Here's the encouraging news: God has given us a healthy option. He wants to help us trade in our unhealthy reactive style for a mature, healthy, and biblically sound way of expressing our secondary emotion of anger in ways that lead to understanding of our primary emotions of fear and/or hurt and/or frustration. God wants to help each of us grow from being a reactor to becoming a mature responder.

THE MATURE RESPONDER

When our buttons get pushed, when we get hurt, when we experience frustration, when fear rears its threatening head, we don't have to react. We don't have to let the situation control us. We don't have to be puppets of our problems or slaves to our circumstances, or give others the power to push our buttons and control the quality of our relationships. With God's help we can choose to respond. It's not as simple as it sounds, but we and many other couples have discovered that it is possible to respond rather than react.

People who have over time become mature responders have learned how to allow God to help them work through their automatic reactions and how to give a healthier, wiser, more thoughtful, and more mature response. This style is not an automatic reaction but involves a learned and reasoned response. It is a way of responding that allows us to be angry without sin (see Ephesians 4:26).

Mature responders have learned how to be responsibly assertive. Unfortunately the word *assertive* is often confused with the word *aggressive.* But there is an enormous difference between the two.

Assertion and aggression are not identical; do not believe any rumors to the contrary. Here's why: Assertion is like having the right of way at the wheel of a late-model Cadillac; aggression is like deliberately plowing into another car at a demolition derby. Aggression is hostile comments or jokes at another's expense; assertion means using humor to defuse a volatile situation diplomatically or to connect to another human being by a shared sense of comedy. Aggression is a disregard for the consequences of your actions; assertion involves taking responsibility. Assertion is freedom from the persistent aggravation of a recurrent problem; aggression re-creates the problems. Assertion is common courtesy; aggression means pushing others around in their own lives.[4]

Mature responders have learned how to speak the truth in love (see Ephesians 4:15). When provoked they are less likely to immediately react without thinking, but rather have trained themselves to respond in ways that reflect some discipline and thought. They understand the difference between unhealthy and healthy anger. They have learned to be aware of their anger. They have learned that anger is an emotion that can provide a wealth of information and can be expressed in healthy and constructive ways.

The anger of those who have never learned to do more than react is characterized by resentment and rage. The anger of the mature responder can be characterized by indignation. What is indignation? How does it differ from rage and resentment? Richard Walters provides a great comparison of these three.

> Rage seeks to do wrong, resentment seeks to hide wrong, indignation seeks to correct wrongs. Rage and resentment seek to destroy people, indignation seeks to destroy evil. Rage and resentment seek vengeance, indignation seeks justice. Rage is guided by selfishness, resentment is guided by cowardice, and indignation is guided by mercy. Rage uses open warfare, resentment is a guerrilla fighter, indignation is an honest and fearless and forceful defender of truth. Rage defends itself, resentment defends the status quo,

indignation defends the other person. Rage and resentment are forbidden by the Bible, indignation is required. . . .

Rage blows up bridges people need to reach each other, and resentment sends people scurrying behind barriers to hide from each other and to hurt each other indirectly. Indignation is constructive: it seeks to heal hurts and to bring people together. Its purpose is to rebuild the bridges and pull down the barriers, yet it is like rage and resentment in that the feelings of anger remain.[5]

The mature response is a style of responding to anger that can transform our relationships. What are some characteristics of a mature responder?

anger communicated	healthy shame	responds
careful	I win/you win	responsible
caring	indignation	thinks before speaking
clear	interdependent	
constructive	listens	trusting
direct communication	motivated by love	unselfish
firm	proactive	warm

So what does a mature responder look like in real life? Rick and Jennifer decided to apply these insights to their own marriage. In this chapter we've seen that although they were deeply in love, like all normal couples there were some aspects of their personalities that triggered anger in each other. It took Jennifer a while to acknowledge that anger is a gift from God and not inherently bad. One of her most powerful anger myths had been that all anger is sinful. She began to see that the real problem wasn't her anger; it was the unhealthy ways she reacted to it. She decided to ask God to help her move from being a cream puff to a mature responder.

It was helpful for her to realize that her anger was a secondary emotion that signaled something was wrong. She knew that one of her most sensitive anger triggers was Rick's tendency to be late. She couldn't figure out why she felt anger every time he came home late. As she thought about it she realized that her secondary emotion of anger was really a response to her primary emotions of hurt and frustration.

Jennifer decided that she had been passive long enough. She needed to be proactive and communicate her concerns to Rick regardless of his reaction. She knew that if there was to be any change she had to work on a way to speak the truth in love (see Ephesians 4:15). After working on it for several weeks, here's what she said to him:

"Rick, in the past two weeks there have been four times that you have been at least twenty minutes late for dinner without calling and letting me know. Every weeknight I work hard at preparing a nice dinner and I look forward to our family time together. When you are late I have to keep it warm and that often affects how it tastes. Your being late also throws everyone else off their schedule. When you are late the message to our family is that we're not important enough for you to be on time and that is disappointing and hurtful. I also feel frustrated that the rest of the family has to pay for your lack of consideration and we are robbed of precious family time. I would appreciate it if you would follow through on your commitment to be home by five forty-five every weeknight. I will have dinner on the table and be ready to eat by six. If you are going to be late please call and let me know. If I don't hear from you, we will go ahead with dinner and you can eat when you get home."

Rick was surprised by the clarity and directness of Jennifer's confrontation. "Wow," he said, "I didn't know you could do that." By choosing to respond with direct communication, in a warm yet firm manner, Jennifer made it easier for Rick to hear what she had to say. She felt understood, Rick felt that he had a much better understanding of her heart and her perspective, and Rick's on-time performance improved significantly.

SMALL BEGINNINGS

Few people express their anger in only one style. However, most people more consistently respond in one style than the other two.

Below we've listed some of the main distinctives of the passive reactor (cream puff), the aggressive reactor (locomotive), and the assertive responder. (The steel magnolia isn't listed below, but it's really a combination of the cream puff and the locomotive.) Read through each one of the lists and ask yourself, "In the past three months how have I expressed my anger?" "What percentage has been passive, aggressive, and assertive?"

THREE STYLES OF DEALING WITH ANGER

Cream Puff (Passive)	Mature Responder (Assertive)	Locomotive (Aggressive)
cold	warm	hot
soft	firm	hard
shame	claim	blame
avoid	approach	attack
repress/suppress	confess	dump
resentment	indignation	rage
inactive	proactive	reactive
dependent	interdependent	independent
anger in	anger communicated	anger against
may love but not speak truth	speaks truth in love	may speak truth but not in love
over-responsible	responsible	under-responsible
false inferiority	honest self-appraisal	false superiority
motivated by fear	motivated by love	motivated by fear
weak boundaries	appropriate boundaries	rigid boundaries
understate/deny issues	clarify issues	overstate/blur issues
I lose/you win	I win/you win	I win/you lose
values others	values self and others	values self

MAKING ANGER WORK FOR YOU

'm so discouraged," Jim said dejectedly. "I don't know why I keep on trying. I make up my mind that I'm not going to lose my temper again and then some little thing happens and I blow it. I get mad at myself, make the same resolution, and when the next time comes I do the same stupid thing all over again. I'm tired of feeling defeated. I'm not sure I can change my anger pattern."

Jim was a fine man. He loved the Lord, his wife, Donna, and their two children. He was a leader in his church and active in a discipleship ministry. However, for many years Jim had struggled with his limited ability to control his anger. He was an aggressive reactor, and for much of his life his anger had worked against him rather than for him.

Many of us can relate to Jim. We have great intentions and we want to be different, but we find that sometimes change is much easier said than done. It's easy to be sincere about wanting things to be different. It's much more difficult to take the steps to make things different. Changing our deep-seated anger reaction patterns can be especially difficult.

If our anger reactions have produced desired results and given us the short-term relief we want, we will tend to react the same way again. If we are passive reactors we may be afraid of our anger. If we are aggressive reactors we may have become addicted to the power our anger has to numb us to our fear of facing the real issues.

The good news is that with God's help meaningful change is possible. We can learn to make our God-given emotion of anger work for us rather than against us. We can learn how to invest our anger energy in constructive responses rather than spend it in destructive reactions. Jim found out he could make his anger work for him and in the process actually increase his trust and intimacy with Donna. The starting point in the change process is to recognize our need to change and to ask God to help us.

The bad news is that the change won't take place overnight. It's unrealistic to think that a twenty-year pattern can be changed in two weeks. It's like trying to change the course of the Colorado River in the middle of the Grand Canyon rather than at the foot of the Rocky Mountains. Deep-seated reaction patterns take time to change.

We need more than a strong desire and good intentions. We need a plan. In Daniel 1:8, we are told that when the prophet Daniel realized he would be taken as a prisoner of war to Babylon he "purposed in his heart" (NKJV) not to defile himself by eating the meat of King Nebuchadnezzar. And he didn't. Why? Because he *purposed in his heart,* he decided in advance what he wanted to accomplish and what his response would be.

Just like Daniel we can *purpose in our hearts* not to allow our anger to control us, but rather to put our anger as well as our other emotions under God's control. Establishing new patterns of anger is like learning to dance. You may step on a few toes, look silly, and feel awkward, but with a little practice you will begin to develop new responses. Over time those new responses will replace the old reactions and become automatic.

So far we've learned that relationships and intimacy were God's idea. In the beginning God designed us to enjoy an intimate relationship with Him and with each other. Because of our sin and selfishness intimacy has become a lot more difficult than God intended it to be. Understanding is required in order to increase the sense of safety, which leads to the increased trust that is necessary to cultivate the relational soil in which deep levels of intimacy can thrive.

We've also learned that one of the main barriers to intimacy is unhealthy anger expressed in ways that create misunderstanding, decrease safety, weaken trust, and eliminate any hope of intimacy. One of the keys to building intimacy is not to eliminate the God-given emotion of anger, but rather to learn how to listen to the underlying message of our anger and harness the anger-energy in healthy ways that can actually increase our understanding of ourselves and others.

In this chapter we will share seven specific steps we can take to experience the emotion of anger as the gift that God intended it to be and learn to make it work *for* us rather than *against* us in our desire to enjoy a more meaningful and intimate love relationship.

STEP #1:
Identify your specific anger pattern

If you had met Jim at church you wouldn't have considered him to be an angry person. He rarely appears to be angry. As we discussed in chapter 6, one of the many anger myths is that if a person doesn't look or appear to be angry then they don't have a problem with anger. While Jim doesn't appear to be an angry person on the outside, he would describe himself as a battlefield on the inside. When he feels misunderstood by Donna or when she contradicts him in public, his anger is right there.

Anger is such a powerful emotion that we must not wait until we are in the midst of it to ponder our response. The best time to begin to deal with anger is *before* we get angry. That's right! Before we experience anger we can study and learn from our past experience. We can identify aspects of our anger reactions that will help us to change. It doesn't matter if they have been successes or failures. God can use both kinds of experiences to help us grow.

As you look at your anger history, answer the following questions:

1. What are the anger myths (chapter 6) that have influenced your misunderstanding of this important emotion? Where did they come from? Do you still function as if they were true?

2. What is your current anger style? Do you tend to be a passive reactor, an aggressive reactor, or a passive-aggressive reactor? What specific behaviors characterize your usual reaction?

3. What kinds of situations are most likely to bring out your anger? Does your anger manifest itself in different ways under different circumstances? How do you react when someone cuts you off, when you're running late and get a flat tire, when the kids are out of control, or when you've worked hard on a particular job and get criticized for the one thing you didn't do?

4. When are you most likely to experience anger? In the morning, afternoon, or evening? After a hard day at work? After a major success or victory?

5. How do you know when you are angry? How do your spouse and kids know when you're angry? What are the warning signs? Does your tone of voice change? Do you speak slower or faster, louder or softer? Do you start to use certain words or expressions such as "I've had it"? Does your heart beat faster? Do you

feel a knot in your stomach? Does some muscle in your body begin to twitch or tighten up?

6. What have you tried in the past that hasn't worked? Our favorite definition of crazy is "to find out what doesn't work and keep on doing it." If the ways in which you are dealing with your anger aren't producing healthy results, then change them.

7. What will be the consequences of not working on your anger? Count the cost of unhealthy anger. One person I worked with brought in the following list of consequences for not changing her anger pattern: Unhealthy anger limits my understanding, hinders my growth, gives Satan an opportunity, allows problems I could have solved to grow into problems that are much more complex, keeps people away, encourages shallow relationships, and affects my physical health.

Our answers to these questions will give us a gold mine of information about how we deal with anger in general and especially how it impacts our marriage relationship. Jim found that Step #1 was a real eye-opener. As he looked at his specific anger pattern he realized that growing up he had learned the anger myth that says the best way to deal with anger is to dump it, just get it out of your system. This contributed to his tendency to be an aggressive reactor (a locomotive). He also discovered that he was most likely to fly off the handle when he was under a lot of pressure or at the end of the day when he came home from work.

Jim realized his anger began with frustration and irritation, then he became aware of a churning in his stomach, an increase in his heartbeat, and a tendency to speak more quickly. Donna and the kids told him they could tell he was starting to get angry because he would butt in and complete their sentences, talk faster and louder, and use more gestures. He then would become more negative, critical, and sarcastic. If things didn't change he would lose it and verbally attack someone. Here is what Jim's anger curve looked like:[1]

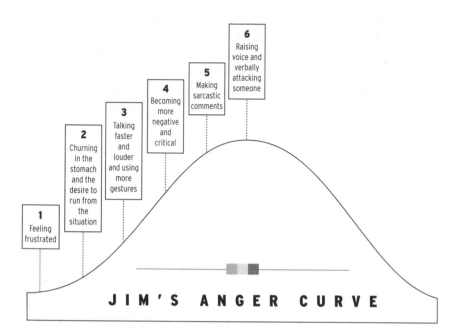

1 Feeling frustrated

2 Churning in the stomach and the desire to run from the situation

3 Talking faster and louder and using more gestures

4 Becoming more negative and critical

5 Making sarcastic comments

6 Raising voice and verbally attacking someone

JIM'S ANGER CURVE

By identifying his fairly common pattern, Jim was able to see signs that alerted him to his anger and thus allowed him to move on to Step #2. Over a period of several months he developed the skill of catching his anger more quickly, often at stage two or three, and dealing with it before it got out of hand.

STEP #2:
Admit your anger and accept responsibility for it

When we are angry it is easy for us to blame someone else, to say "It's your fault. You made me angry." Adam and Eve did it, and we do it. This is *especially* true in marriage. We can blame our spouse, our children, our boss, our friends, the weather, the mechanic, people we know, or people we have never met.

While it is true that other people can say or do things that influence our experience of anger, *we are responsible* for how we *choose* to express it. If we are angry it is *our* anger, not someone else's. What we do with our anger is our *choice*.

When we admit our anger and accept responsibility for it, we are saying, "I am angry. I can't control the fact that I am experiencing anger. But with God's help I can control how I *choose* to express my anger."

In Psalm 139:23–24, David writes, "Search me, O God, and know my heart; test me and know my anxious thoughts. See if there is any offensive way in me, and lead me in the way everlasting." David takes personal responsibility for what he needs to do. Notice he doesn't say "Search my wife" or "Try my spouse's heart." He says search *me,* test *me,* and lead *me.*

As Jim became more aware of when and why he was angry, he found it easier to admit it and accept responsibility for it. This helped to reinforce in his mind the difference between the experience of anger and the expression of anger. Up until this point he had functioned as if his experience and expression of anger were the same thing and he had no choice. As he better understood his experience of anger, he became more aware of his freedom to choose healthy ways to express it.

As Jim increasingly admitted and accepted responsibility for his anger this led to a decrease in his tendency to blame Donna and the kids. We often begin a counseling session with the question "What's been a little bit better since the last time we met?" Jim was surprised when Donna responded to that question with "Over the past few weeks the kids and I have noticed that Jim isn't blaming us as much." We could tell that this had been a very meaningful change. "How has that been helpful to you?" I asked. "Well," Donna said, "I hadn't really thought about that, but I guess the more I hear him take responsibility and not blame me, the safer I feel around him and the easier it is for me to trust him."

STEP #3:
Determine who or what
is going to have control

When we become aware that we are angry we are faced with a critical choice that will determine everything else. We can either allow the emotion of anger to dominate and control us or we can, with the help of the Holy Spirit, *choose* to control the anger and invest the anger energy in healthy ways. Often we may have only a matter of seconds to make that choice, but it is nonetheless a choice. While we can't always control when we experience anger, we can with God's help choose how we express the anger. As we choose to take our anger to God in prayer, He will help us find creative and constructive ways to deal with it.

When we allow any emotion to be in control it interferes with our learning, narrows our perception, and causes us to have tunnel vision. It hinders our ability to do creative problem-solving, limits our ability to recall what we have learned, wastes time and energy, increases our vulnerability to other problems, and leads to impulsive behavior. Any emotion that we allow to control us will become problem-causing rather than problem-solving.

One of the best ways to stay in control is to take time to process our anger. Ecclesiastes 7:9 says, "Do not be quickly provoked in your spirit, for anger resides in the lap of fools." James adds, "Be quick to listen, slow to speak and slow to become angry, for man's anger does not bring about the righteous life that God desires" (James 1:19–20). In advance, we can determine to be slow to express our anger and delay action.

Delay is the greatest remedy for unhealthy anger. If we are in the middle of an argument with our spouse, we may need to take a timeout. We can always say, "I know this issue is important, but I'm feeling some strong emotions, and I need some time to sort out my thoughts." When angry, count to ten before speaking. (If you are really angry, count to one hundred, and then don't say anything for twenty-four hours.)

STEP #4:
Define it and identify the cause or source of it

Harriet Lerner writes, "It is amazing how frequently we march off to battle without knowing what the war is all about. We may be putting our anger energy into trying to change or control a person who does not want to change rather than putting that same energy into getting clear about our own position and choices."[2]

We can get clear about our position by identifying our secondary emotion of anger and the primary emotion or emotions that are the real source. While there are an almost limitless number of situations that can lead to anger, remember what we learned in chapter 5, that the secondary emotion of anger usually comes from the primary emotions of hurt and/or frustration and/or fear.

Hurt is usually caused by something that has already happened . . . something in the past. When we are hurt we feel vulnerable to even more hurt. We feel at risk. This is especially true of people who are very sensitive. Believe it or not, even men can be sensitive. When he was growing up, Jim's dad said hurtful things that made Jim feel weak and foolish. Jim says, "I now understand that anger gave me a sense of power and I didn't feel quite as weak and vulnerable."

For many of us anger is an automatic defense mechanism to protect against hurt. Dealing with hurt can drain us of energy and make us feel even more vulnerable. The energy we get from our anger can give us the strength to fight back with the person who caused the pain.

When we get angry at someone it tends to erect a wall between us and then we can hide behind that wall. The unhealthy expression of anger produces distance between individuals, and many feel safer with that distance. What are some of the hurts in your life that have led to the emotion of anger?

Frustration is an emotion that takes place in the present. We can become frustrated by blocked goals or desires or by unmet expectations. Frequently the things that lead to the greatest frustrations have one main characteristic: they really aren't that important. However, at the time they appear to be huge.

In our marriage, one situation that has frequently led to my (Gary's) expressing unhealthy anger is when I'm trying to communicate with Carrie and she doesn't seem to get what I'm trying to say. I can get frustrated, and I've discovered that I'm especially vulnerable to frustration when I'm tired and in a hurry. When Carrie doesn't seem to get it, I can have what seems like an automatic and even unconscious interpretation that she's intentionally not trying or not listening, or she just doesn't care. When that happens, I can get even more frustrated and react by becoming sarcastic, cold, and critical. I'm not proud of it, I don't enjoy it, I've apologized on numerous occasions for it, and I've made great progress with it—but from time to time it still happens.

Reflect on what frustrates you and what causes you to get frustrated with your spouse. What situations or individuals have frustrated you this past month? When are you most vulnerable to experiencing frustration? How do you usually react when you are frustrated?

Fear is an emotion that tends to focus on things in the future. Many people associate fear with vulnerability and weakness. Some people, especially men, find it more comfortable to express anger than fear, and so many respond to situations in which they are anxious or afraid by getting angry. When you are experiencing the emotion of anger and aren't sure where it's coming from, ask yourself, "Is there something that I'm afraid of that could be triggering my anger?"

When one newlywed couple we worked with had an argument, the wife would threaten to leave him and go back to live with her mother. The husband's immediate reaction was an angry one in which he would remind her of all of her failures and shortcomings and basically say that maybe that would be the best thing for her to do. "But," he said with a note of deep sadness, "that's not what I really want."

After several sessions he realized that one of his greatest fears was losing his wife. "When she talks about walking out I feel attacked, threatened, and afraid that I'll lose her. It feels like I've been punched in the stomach. My almost unconscious reaction is to attack her back, to make her feel bad for how bad I feel. But then I feel bad about what I've said." Over time he saw how his reaction only made things worse for both of them.

She saw how her initial angry reaction was in part due to her fear that he would never really want to take the time to understand her and care for her. During their fights what they both wanted was to be understood and loved. But their unhealthy anger reaction to their fears was to push each other's buttons in ways that destroyed any hope of intimacy.

The secondary emotion of anger is hard to deal with because frequently we are dealing with a symptom of another problem. If we allow God to help us identify the root cause or causes of our anger, we are well on the way to harnessing the positive potential of healthy anger in building bridges of understanding in our marriage relationship.

STEP #5:
If a response is appropriate, choose your response

Remember that one of the positive functions of anger is that it can serve as a warning or alarm system. The only problem is that sometimes it is a false alarm. When our anger alarm goes off, how can we determine if it is a legitimate alarm or a false alarm? What's the difference?

Scott and Andrea are a busy couple but have worked hard at making their marriage and family a priority. Andrea's division at work was facing a big deadline. Tuesday night was their usual family night, but on Monday her boss had told her she would have to work late. That evening she prepared a special dish and asked Scott if, when he got home from work on Tuesday, he would put it in the oven so it would be ready when she got home.

Monday had been a rough day and Tuesday was even worse. All the way home Andrea looked forward to a great home-cooked meal and some relaxing time with her family. When she walked in the door she didn't smell any food cooking, the table wasn't set, and Scott and the kids were sitting in the family room watching TV.

Andrea lost it. "I can't believe it!" she shouted. "I stayed up late last night to prepare a good meal, and the only thing you had to do was put it in the oven. Give me a break! Is that too much to ask? I'm sick and tired of doing all the work while you guys sit around and do nothing!" Andrea was obviously angry. Her interpretation of the situation led to feelings of hurt and frustration, which in turn produced her anger.

Unfortunately her anger was a false alarm. She misinterpreted what she saw. After she unloaded, Scott told her that he had decided to surprise her. He thought that after a long, hard day she might enjoy going out for dinner with the family. Then there would be no dishes to wash and no kitchen to clean up. He had the best of intentions. The kids were excited to go out, and he thought Andrea would be pleasantly surprised. With this new information Andrea's anger immediately disappeared and she apologized to Scott and the kids.

Here are a few questions that can help you determine whether your anger is a false alarm or the real thing: Is my anger due to real problems or to unrealistic expectations? Is my interpretation accurate or is my perspective distorted? Am I taking things too seriously? Have I assumed the other person intentionally did this? If an outside observer saw this would he view my response as warranted, appropriate, and reasonable? How much control do I have over the situation? If you can't control it or influence it, you can do nothing about it.

Let's return to Jim. As he defined his anger and identified its source, he discovered that at least 50 percent of the time his anger was a false alarm. Because of his tendency to overgeneralize and jump to negative conclusions, it was easy for him to be caught off guard by a comment or situation, assume the worst, and ventilate his anger. He realized the importance of checking out and clarifying interpretations and perceptions before responding.

If we discover that our anger is a false alarm, or it is a situation we can't control or influence, we probably don't need to respond. By not reacting we save time and energy and possibly avoid some word or deed that we might have regretted.

If it *is* a situation that demands a response, we have to *choose* how to respond. In order to make this decision we need to determine how important the issue is. Here's a quick and simple way to make this decision: On a scale from one to ten, with one being low and ten being high, how would you rate it? If it's one through five it's a low-ticket issue. If it's a six through ten it's a high-ticket issue.

One of the many problems with the reactive anger styles is that the reaction to a situation is often disproportionate to the significance of the situation. Reactors treat high-ticket issues as if they were low-ticket or vice versa. Thus neither they nor those around them are able to discern what's really important and what isn't.

Imagine that our anger-energy is like cash, and every day we are given ten dollars to spend. Is this situation worth spending six dollars' worth of our limited anger-energy? Or is it only a two-dollar issue? We wouldn't spend eight dollars for a pack of gum, yet we often waste valuable energy over comparatively insignificant issues. With some practice, over time we can learn to spend what the situation is worth, no more and no less.

If it is a high-ticket issue, then we will want to be more careful in choosing our response. We can ask ourselves, "What is my primary emotion and how can I express it in a way that is biblically consistent and that will lead to greater understanding? What do I really want to communicate? What do I hope will happen as a result of communicating my hurt or frustration or fear? How can I convey the information in such a way that the other person can accept it and that it will benefit him or her?"

It is helpful to ask, "What is the issue from the other person's perspective? If I were the other person, how might I respond if someone said this to me in this way? What will make it easier for him or her to hear my real message? What has or hasn't worked in the past?"

We can either spend or invest our anger-energy. The cream puff is likely to spend it by attacking herself. The locomotive is likely to spend it by attacking someone else. In both cases there are no winners. Everyone loses! When we spend our anger-energy the results are almost always destructive.

When anger-energy is invested it often leads to relational healing. We can determine whether our response will hurt or heal. Before we go any further we can choose to set aside the destructive responses. This involves saying to ourselves, "With God's help I choose not to hide or hurl my anger by jumping to conclusions, attacking, blaming, lecturing, labeling, dumping, preaching, demoralizing, ridiculing, humiliating, bossing, or manipulating the other person."

STEP #6:
Just do it!

Step six is where we apply what we've learned to a specific situation. Sounds easy, doesn't it? Well, it may be simple, but for most people it isn't easy, especially in the beginning. It's much easier to talk about change than it is to actually do it. We're often surprised to find out how powerful our habits can be. But go ahead. Do it. If you make a mistake you can learn from it. It won't take long to discover that healthy anger can give you the energy to deal with the source of your anger in ways that can lead to understanding and even resolution.

As you begin to change your reactive pattern you may discover, as many others have, that what you thought was an issue is no longer an issue. There is no longer a need to share your primary emotion or confront another person. However, if the problem continues and if you need to confront an issue with someone, pray about it, choose a time that will be good for both of you, rehearse what you are going to say in advance, and do it. The longer you put off sharing your hurt, frustration, or fear, or mending a quarrel, the more difficult it will be to deal with. Don't allow a misunderstanding to fester.

Norman Wright says that confrontation isn't a vindictive attack or an argument, and it's not intended to alienate or change anyone. It is simply a sharing of facts and feelings. Confrontation isn't about releasing or dumping your anger on someone. "You don't confront someone to punish him, get even with him, frighten him, or make him suffer."[3] In fact, as you move through these seven steps you will have already dealt with much of your secondary emotion of anger and the primary emotions that were its source.

Healthy confrontation is a way of bringing a problem out into the open where it can be defined, understood, and dealt with. Healthy confrontation is a constructive way to deal with an issue that would continue to fester if it was not openly discussed and dealt with.

Let's see what these steps look like in the real-life example of Jim and Donna. We encouraged Jim and Donna to pick a comparatively low-ticket issue to practice the steps. Jim decided he wanted to work on his tendency to overreact whenever he perceived Donna to be criticizing him in public. Their actual conversation took close to thirty minutes, but here is a step-by-step summary.

In the first part of this chapter, we saw that Jim identified himself as an aggressive reactor, and this was the first step. Over time he learned to admit when he was angry and take responsibility, and relationally, this proved to be a significant second step. He took the third step when he decided that he was no longer going to allow his anger to control him, but that with God's help he was going to understand his anger and make it work for him rather than against him. Step four he had already done: He identified that one of the things that triggered his anger was his hurt and frustration over being criticized by Donna in public. Although she said her intention wasn't to be critical, it still was hurtful and frustrating.

In step five, Jim decided that while this wasn't a high-ticket issue, it was something that occurred with some degree of frequency, and it would be an issue worth confronting. He decided the best response would be to share his primary emotions and concern with Donna by making an appointment to talk with her.

In step six, Jim acknowledged that while Donna's intention wasn't to be critical of him and embarrass him, there were times when he felt criticized, embarrassed, and even humiliated, and that this caused him to feel hurt and frustrated. He shared a couple of specific times when that had happened. While Donna was surprised to discover how that felt to him, she was able to accept the fact that her behavior wasn't helpful. She told him that she was more than willing to change. They ended their conversation with a short word of prayer, thanking God for His love for them, for helping them through what even a few months earlier would have been an impossible conversation, and for the strength to continue growing in their understanding and love for each other.

STEP #7:
Review it!

The review process doesn't take long. Start by thanking God for His love and His faithfulness in this situation. Then ask yourself,

"What worked and what didn't work? What went better and what didn't? What did I learn? How have I grown? What can I do differently that will help me to be more effective next time? Do I better understand my spouse or do I feel better understood by him or her?"

As we invited Jim and Donna to review their interaction, Donna was the first to speak: "At first I was surprised that my behavior was so hurtful to him, and after thinking about it I realized how courageous it was for him to make himself vulnerable by sharing that with me." Jim responded by sharing that he had never realized that his anger wasn't really caused by Donna but by the primary emotions caused in part by his own misinterpretations of her comments. "If it hadn't been for this process I would still be *reacting* rather than *responding*." What had been a wall keeping them apart now became a bridge of understanding into each other's hearts.

For many Christians both the experience and the expression of anger have become a habit. Habits can be hard to change, and it may take some time. The good news is that with God's help we can change, we can grow, and we can become more than conquerors. Through the power of the Holy Spirit and the promises in God's Word we can take old dysfunctional and unhealthy ways of reacting and develop new, healthy, and biblically consistent emotional responses.

How do you know if you are changing? Remember that change takes time and often involves two steps forward and one step backward. Don't be discouraged by the setbacks. They are a normal part of the growth process and can provide invaluable feedback. Setbacks can lead to new insights and fresh motivation for continued growth and learning.

When our anger patterns are influenced by the promises and principles of God's Word we will still have problems, but those problems will not dominate or devastate us. Rather they will be able to be used of God to help us develop into the man or woman of His design.

David Augsburger offers three helpful suggestions for dealing with anger:

1. BE angry, but beware: You are never more vulnerable than when you are angry. Self-control is at an all-time low, reason decreases, common sense leaves.
2. BE angry, but be aware: Anger can easily turn into resentment, bitterness, and violence. Anger can become a way of life, making you bitter and joyless.
3. BE angry but be kind: Only when anger is motivated by love is it constructive and creative anger.[4]

SMALL BEGINNINGS

1. What is your anger pattern? What does your anger curve look like? (Below is an anger curve you can fill out for yourself.) While it may not be exactly the same for every situation, most people have fairly consistent patterns.

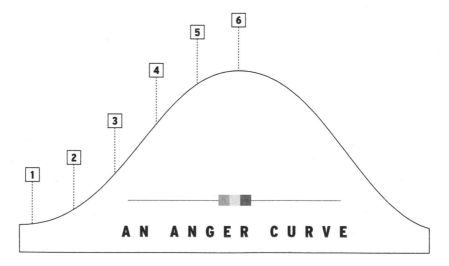

AN ANGER CURVE

2. Do you tend to blame others for your secondary emotion of anger? How can you take responsibility for your anger? What would that look like?

3. Have you taken your anger to God in prayer and asked Him to help you control it rather than your anger controlling you?

4. Was hurt, fear, or frustration the underlying emotion the last time you experienced the secondary emotion of anger? Or was it a combination of them? If you were forced to pick the one most frequent primary emotion behind your anger, which one would it be? Which one would your spouse or your kids pick?

5. Can you think of a time when your anger was a false alarm? What can you learn from the situation that will help you to more effectively identify false alarms in the future?

6. Is there a hurt, frustration, or fear that you need to share with your spouse that might help him or her better understand you? Which one would be easiest for you to share? How could you share it in a way that would make it easiest for your spouse to receive it?

7. How could you confront your spouse about an issue in a healthy way? Think of a time when you have confronted your spouse in the past and it has gone well. What made it more effective? Would you have the courage to ask him or her? Would you have the courage to ask your spouse if there is a hurt, frustration, or fear he or she would like to share with you or a low-ticket (remember, that's always the best place to start) issue he or she would like you to better understand?

INTIMATE CONFLICT: A PATHWAY TO INTIMACY

Before meeting Carrie I had been to London several times as a single student, but this was the first time we would be there together. We were on our way to Amsterdam to begin a two-week tour of Europe and had two days to spend in London. That was the good news.

The bad news was that we arrived just days before the royal wedding was to take place. I had never seen London so packed. The city was jammed with people from all over the world. But even more interesting was the uncharacteristic spirit of optimism in the air. People had been captivated by the magical courtship and romance of Prince Charles and Lady Diana and were excited about the wedding.

Three days later the couple walked down the aisle and stood in front of Robert Runcie, Archbishop of Canterbury. He looked Prince Charles and Lady Diana in the eyes and in a warm yet solemn voice said, "Here is the stuff of which fairy tales are made, the prince and princess on their wedding day. But fairy tales usually end at this point with the simple phrase 'They lived happily ever after.' This may be because fairy tales regard marriage as an anticlimax after the romance of courtship. This is not the Christian view. Our faith sees the wedding day not as a place of arrival but the place where the adventure begins."

We will never know if Charles and Diana even heard what the archbishop had to say or if they took it to heart. We do know that the fairy-tale wedding turned into a painful soap opera with a tragic ending. It's also a great tragedy that far too many couples see their wedding day as a place of arrival and not as the place where the real adventure and thus the real work begins.

Like most other couples, Carrie and I discovered that marriage, especially in its first year, is a relationship that demands flexibility, adjustments, and change. Not necessarily major personality reconstruction, but certainly numerous minor adjustments and fine-tunings. Unless people look at their marriage vows as a daily opportunity to choose to grow, they are in for some increasingly difficult times and will grow apart, never achieving the intimacy and trust they both desire.

Research tells us that one of the main problems that plagues marriages is unresolved conflict. It started long ago in the garden of Eden with Adam and Eve, and it's been going on ever since. We don't understand it. Most of us don't like it. It's been said that there's only one thing people avoid more than change, and that's conflict. If you think about it, that's not too surprising, since conflict is frequently an inevitable part of the change and growth process.

What do you think of when you hear the word *conflict*? Is your first reaction positive or negative? Most of us have a negative view of conflict because of the way our parents dealt with it. But conflict can be positive when we deal with it in a healthy way.

It took us many years to learn the value of healthy conflict. Both Carrie and I grew up in homes where conflict was avoided. We went into our marriage with the assumption that conflict was negative and should be avoided, and when it can't be avoided it should be dealt with in ways that bring peace and harmony as quickly as possible. We viewed it as a rude and unwelcome interruption in our lives rather than a normal and necessary part of growing a deep, trusting, and intimate love relationship.

When we began to turn to the Bible to see what it had to say about dealing with conflict, we were surprised to discover that conflict is a major theme in the Bible. From Genesis to Revelation we find man and woman in conflict with God, themselves, and each other. Conflict is the process we go through and the price we pay for intimacy. After twenty-six years of marriage and over fifty years of combined experience as marriage counselors, we've discovered that intimacy is always achieved at the price of listening, facing our differences and negative emotions, understanding them, and resolving them.

One of the things that helped us turn a major corner in dealing with conflict was the discovery that most conflict develops through predictable stages. If you and your spouse can identify and understand the underlying patterns that lead to conflict, you are much more likely to be able to make conflict work *for* you rather than against you.

STAGE #1:
Differences

When Dale first met Liz, he was attracted to her fun-loving, extroverted style. She loved to talk with people and had a way of drawing him out. Liz was attracted to Dale because he seemed like "the strong, silent, thoughtful type. He was so different from all the other guys I had dated." So far so good. As with most couples, the differences they encountered early in the relationship were acceptable and even intriguing.

In Romans, we are encouraged to "be of the same mind" (12:16 NKJV), to "accept one another" (15:7), and to "admonish one another" (15:14 NKJV). This is especially applicable in marriage. Marriage involves two people coming together. However, as we seek to become one in Christ we find that our differences can produce problems. They can lead to disagreements that at times result in conflict.

People are attracted to each other because of the uniqueness they see in each other. They marry because they believe they can be happier with that person than without him or her. But couples have conflict because the unique qualities that initially attracted them quickly become differences that frustrate, depress, and discourage them. People fight because the unique person they thought they couldn't live without has opinions and habits they believe they would be much happier living without. Spouses separate because they have given up hope of their partner becoming the person they thought they married and/or the person they think their partner needs to become if they are to be happy.

Our differences—when understood, appreciated, and allowed to be used by God—can actually enrich our lives and our marriage relationships. Our differences are like instruments in an orchestra. Before

THE CONFLICT & INTIMACY CYCLE

Differences

the concert begins, while the various instruments are warming up and being tuned, the sound is atrocious. However, when the conductor raises his or her baton and the musicians begin to play, the trumpet, oboe, French horn, violin, trombone, flute, tuba, and bassoon come together to produce a beautiful sound that would be impossible with only one instrument. The real beauty of an orchestra comes as we learn to blend the music of our instruments in ways that create harmony. The beauty of a relationship shows when we learn to blend the music of two personalities to create relational harmony.

God wants to use our differences to conform us to the image of His Son or, as Proverbs puts it, to "sharpen" one another (27:17). What do you get when iron rubs against iron? Heat. Sparks fly. But if the pieces are rubbed in the right way, they inevitably sharpen each other and they become more useful. Marriage is the most significant relationship that God will use to refine, shape, and sharpen us in the process of becoming more like himself.

This process of rubbing lives together day after day, month after month, year after year becomes God's change agent, His refining tool to make us better people, to rub off the rough edges of our personalities, to help us understand our own emotions and when we can and can't trust them, to give us understanding hearts, to teach us acceptance, to help us change. This change will occur if we choose to learn from each other. But if we remain rigid, we will thwart one of the great purposes of marriage.

Churches are not destroyed by differences. Families are not destroyed by differences. Marriages are not destroyed by differences. They are destroyed by the immature, irresponsible, and unhealthy ways we choose to respond to those differences. They are destroyed by our inability or unwillingness to take them to God and allow Him to use them for His glory.

DIFFERENCES THAT LEAD TO CONFLICT

Remember, conflict arises because every human being is different. Stop for just a moment and think about you and your spouse.

1. What are some of the ways in which you are different?

    Do you come from different ethnic backgrounds?

    Were you raised in different parts of the country?

    How were your childhoods different?

    Did one grow up in the country and another in a large city?

    What were your parents like?

    How many brothers and sisters did you have?

    Where were you in the birth order? Oldest, middle child, youngest?

    What are your personality types?

    How are your personalities similar and how are they different?

    Is one of you more introverted and the other more extroverted?

    Is one of you organized and structured and the other spontaneous and random?

2. What might God be wanting you to learn through those differences? How can they be seen as complementary and not merely contradictory?

STAGE #2:
Disagreement

It usually doesn't take much time after the wedding for our spouse's personality traits and habits that we thought were special to become frustrating, confusing, and just plain wrong. Relationships involve people coming together, but because we are all different disagreement is inevitable.

While they were dating, Dale and Liz bumped into some differences, but the excitement of romantic love felt so good they chose to gloss over them. For a while they were able to successfully ignore them. However, after they were married they found themselves disagreeing more and more. As what had been comfortable differences became uncomfortable, they found themselves at Stage #2 of the Intimacy Cycle. The differences they had only partially understood and had chosen to ignore during courtship were becoming a problem. Wow! What a difference a wedding can make.

THE CONFLICT & INTIMACY CYCLE

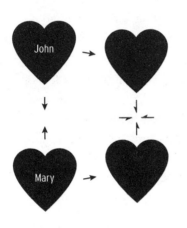

Differences → Disagreement

Eventually Dale and Liz's differences led to disagreements they could no longer ignore. Unfortunately, neither one of them grew up in a home where they learned healthy styles of conflict resolution. It didn't take them long to develop a dance that they were able to identify only after several years. It went something like this:

1. Liz shares an emotion or feeling. Dale feels threatened or criticized and challenges the logic of her feeling, or he hears what Liz says as a message that he needs to be responsible and tries to fix the problem.
2. Liz tries again.
3. Dale feels like he has failed to understand or help her, so he withdraws to avoid his rising anger or discomfort.

4. Liz's frustration leads to anger that she expresses by criticizing Dale, trying to draw him out. She continues to push Dale to get him to interact with her.

5. Dale starts criticizing her as a way to protect himself, and in his anger he calls her names and shames her.

6. Liz feels put down, and Dale feels rejected and unhappy with his own behavior, but he isn't willing to admit it or be vulnerable.

7. One of them loses it and attacks the other with generalizations such as "You always . . ." or "You never . . ." or "You're just like your mother (or father)."

8. The situation is so disappointing and painful that their fear of conflict and belief that nothing good can ever come from conflict is reinforced and they simply work harder to stuff, suppress, repress, deny, and ignore problems until, once again, they grow to the point of threatening the relationship.

Dale and Liz (and most other couples) didn't spend much time in Stage #2. Once we start to disagree we almost immediately move into Stage #3.

STAGE #3:
The Wall of Conflict

In Stage #3, couples hit the wall of conflict. When we hit the wall, our immediate reaction is to run at it or run away, to attack or avoid, fight or flight. In this stage, many men feel threatened by their own vulnerability and the increasingly assertive behavior of their wives. Unhealthy and out-of-control anger can take center stage, and the issues that led to the conflict are forgotten in the wake of the deeper fears and anxieties they have struggled with for years.

THE CONFLICT & INTIMACY CYCLE

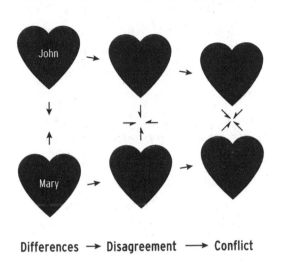

Differences → Disagreement ⟶ Conflict

Dale and Liz did what many couples do. They cycled back to Stage #1 and started the process all over again. They would have several hours or days of silence and then kiss and make up and pretend that everything was fine. Nothing was clearly identified or resolved. They'd lost another opportunity to explore, understand, and learn from their differences. When Dale and Liz started marriage counseling, a light came on for Dale. He realized, "We've been doing this silly dance for years. And we always end up right back where we started."

"You're right," I replied. "Do you want to continue to do that dysfunctional dance?" I asked. They both blurted out an emphatic "No!" I went on to tell them that with help and over time we can learn to break through the wall of conflict and move to Stage #4 to *achieve understanding, growth, and resolution that produces change.* However, if they were to do this they would need to do two things.

First of all, they would need to reframe their view of conflict from something that is always negative and destructive to a positive opportunity for growth in their relationship. Second, they would need to identify their dysfunctional styles of dealing with conflict and replace them with healthy styles.

Before reading any further ask yourself these questions: What is your immediate reaction to conflict at work? With your spouse? With your kids? With your friends? Does conflict make you comfortable or uncomfortable? How well have your conflict management skills worked for you in your relationships?

UNDERSTANDING THE VALUE OF HEALTHY CONFLICT

Both Dale and Liz had a negative view of conflict. He came from a home in which conflict was avoided. She came from a home where she saw all kinds of conflict, but little of it was healthy. "I never dreamed that conflict could be constructive," Dale observed. In fact, of the literally thousands of couples we have worked with, we've yet to meet one who grew up with a healthy perspective of conflict. Not one!

I reached into my desk drawer and pulled out a handout I give couples titled "12 Insights for Healthy Conflict." I'll let you read them for yourself:

1. Conflict is a natural phenomenon and is inevitable. An occupational hazard of being human is that we will experience conflict.
2. Conflict involves both personal needs and relationship needs. (We'll explain this further later in this chapter.)
3. Most conflict is not dealt with openly because most people have not been taught effective ways of resolving conflict. When there is conflict most of us tend to personalize it, interpret it as an attack, and magnify negative implications of statements.
4. Conflict provides opportunities for growth in a relationship.
5. Unresolved conflicts interfere with growth and satisfying relationships. Problems don't magically disappear. They go underground and grow and develop into other problems.

6. As we understand the value of conflict, we can allow it to serve a more positive and constructive role in our lives.

7. The more we try to deny, hide from, overlook, and otherwise avoid conflict, the greater the problem becomes.

8. It is normal to feel defensive when challenged or criticized, thus conflict often involves anger.

9. Conflict isn't good or bad, right or wrong . . . conflict simply is. It is how we choose to respond to conflict that produces the growth or creates the real problem.

10. If we want conflict to serve a constructive role in our lives, pursuing healthy conflict must become a priority.

11. Constructive conflict involves a commitment to serve one another, encourage one another, and be vulnerable with one another. In the early stages it involves caring enough to be willing to take some risks.

12. Constructive conflict involves a commitment to stop, look, listen, and then, maybe, speak.

PERSONAL NEEDS VS. RELATIONSHIP NEEDS

Whenever two people disagree there are always at least *two levels of needs*. First of all, we have our personal needs. Part of the reason we have conflict is that each spouse thinks or wants something different. On their honeymoon Dale wanted to get to the destination and then enjoy himself. His goal was to arrive at the hotel at the time they had planned. On the other hand, Liz wasn't too concerned about when they got to the hotel. She wanted to enjoy the trip there. She thought it might be fun to explore some shops along the way, look for a quaint restaurant, and talk.

While Dale and Liz had different personal needs, they also had a need to nurture their relationship. Dale said, "I knew it was important for me to deal with this issue in a way that wouldn't seriously injure our relationship." That of course is the challenge of effective conflict resolution. How can we deal with issues in ways that take into account our *personal* and *relationship* needs while at the same time honoring those of our spouse?

FOUR CONFLICT STYLES

There are four styles of dealing with conflict based on how we address our personal and relationship needs.

In Style #1 we *avoid* the conflict completely and walk away. This style says, "I'll get away." We refuse to discuss the situation and stonewall our partner. This style is the least effective because we lose out on both our personal and relationship needs.

In Style #2 we *attack* the other person. This style says, "I'll get what I want or I'll get him or her." We go for control. This was Liz's preferred style. She was bright, verbal, confident, assertive, and competitive. When she wanted something she went for it.

Liz was usually able to confront in ways that were healthy and appropriate, that showed sensitivity and respect for the other person. However, when her sense of significance or security was challenged or threatened, she would go for the win. Her motto was "Take no captives." She was able to get her personal needs met, but at the cost of the relationship. Over time she learned that, in any relationship, whenever *one* person wins what really happens is that *both* people lose.

Some people whose predominant style is to attack aren't as healthy as Liz was. They always have to win. They always have to be right. They need to see themselves as better, brighter, and more important than anyone else. No matter how much applause, praise, or recognition they get, their needs can never be filled.

While Liz's predominant style was Style #2, to *attack*, Dale's was Style #3, to *acquiesce*. This is the opposite of Style #2. Style #3 says, "I believe in peace at any price so I'll acquiesce, or give in." Those who choose to acquiesce are choosing to give up on their *personal* needs to achieve their *relational* needs of peace and harmony. They may have grown up with the idea that it is never good to make waves or disagree with your spouse. For a while Dale was able to do this. "After all," he said, "the Bible teaches that men are to be peacemakers, and I want to be a godly man." Meeting his *relational* need for harmony was at times more important than getting his *personal* needs met. The only problem is that he could only stuff, repress, suppress, deny, and ignore his personal needs for so long.

These first three styles of approaching conflict are unhealthy and usually toxic, if not destructive, to the relationship. They lead to circular arguments that produce more heat than light, build more walls than bridges, and increase the hurting rather than the healing.

Style #4 is a healthy style that allows us to honor our own and our partner's personal and relationship needs. It involves *approach*. It pursues collaboration. It says, "I'll meet you halfway," and often involves finding some kind of a win-win compromise.

Before going any further we need to make sure you understand that *compromise* is not a dirty word. Many people assume that compromise is merely a synonym for *sell out*. Sometimes that is the case; however, Webster defines *compromise* as an adaptation, an adjustment of differences, or a settlement.

In the context of conflict, compromise means bargaining some personal needs for some relationship needs. Legitimate love always requires a bit of compromise, and in our experience over 90 percent of a couple's conflicts can be dealt with through healthy compromise.

In Style #4 we are able to reach a solution for the immediate problem. Dale and Liz frequently disagreed about what TV shows their kids should watch. With some patience and encouragement they finally developed enough conflict resolution skills that they were able to decide whether their kids should or should not watch a particular program.

The better we become at approaching issues and dealing with conflict, the better we become at reaching levels of understanding that go beyond immediate issues. As we talk, share, listen, and ask questions, we better understand our spouse, child, or friend. We are able to go beyond the specific issue at hand and arrive at an understanding that deals with a whole category of issues.

As Dale and Liz talked about their concerns with various TV programs, their discussion extended to movies. They began to clarify both for themselves and for each other the deeper values that underlay the opinions they expressed. Over the course of several conversations, some of them rather animated, they discovered that not only did they understand each other better, but they had arrived at a mutual policy regarding all movies and TV programs for their kids.

The following chart illustrates the effectiveness of the four styles of conflict and how they impact our intimacy. *Avoiding* conflict is totally ineffective. While the *attack* style meets one's personal needs, it fails to deal with relationship needs. *Acquiescing* meets some short-term relationship needs at the cost of personal needs. When we *approach* we bargain some of our personal needs for our relationship needs and eventually . . . collaborate. We work together to understand the issues behind the conflict. We leave the conflict not only having solved the immediate problem at hand, but with a deeper understanding of and appreciation for each other's perspective.

	PERSONAL NEEDS	RELATION- SHIP NEEDS	INTIMACY
(1) Avoid	-	-	None
(2) Attack	+	-	None
(3) Acquiesce	-	+	None
(4) Approach & Collaborate	+++	+++	High

What is *your* predominant style of conflict resolution? What style was modeled for you in your family of origin? We've seen that Dale grew up with the Acquiesce style and Liz grew up with the Attack style. Which style are you most likely to respond in? If you are like most people, it is one of the first three styles: Avoid, Attack, or Acquiesce. Are you happy with your current style? Has it been effective? Has it increased the understanding, safety, trust, and intimacy in your marriage? If not, are you willing to make a commitment to change, to grow in your ability to effectively deal with conflict?

STAGE #4:
Choose How You Will Interpret It

Whenever we experience conflict we are faced with an important decision: How will we choose to interpret conflict? We can choose to interpret it negatively or positively. The difficult part of this stage is that for most of us our interpretation is subconscious. We don't think about how we're going to interpret the conflict, we just react in whatever way we've reacted for most of our lives. At times it seems like an involuntary choice, something that was hard-wired into our personality at birth.

But our response to conflict isn't involuntary. It wasn't hard-wired into us at birth. We do have a choice, and with God's help we can teach ourselves new and healthier ways to respond. We can choose a problem-focused or a growth-focused interpretation. Our choice will to a great degree determine whether our love relationship will deepen and grow or stagnate. Many years ago we learned that how we *view* conflict will always determine how we *do* conflict. When couples avoid or ignore

THE CONFLICT & INTIMACY CYCLE

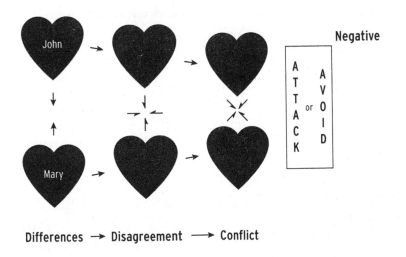

Differences → Disagreement → Conflict

conflict they achieve a delicate, short-lived pseudo-intimacy. It feels good for a while, but it doesn't last long. When couples learn to embrace conflict they can achieve a deep, rich, genuine, and long-lasting intimacy.

THE PROBLEM-FOCUSED (NEGATIVE) INTERPRETATION

Most people choose to see conflict as negative—something to be avoided at all costs. Some believe that one sign of Christian maturity is that everyone always agrees. This distorted perspective interprets conflict as a sign of immaturity and carnality. But someone has said that where everyone always agrees and thinks alike, no one thinks very much at all.

> *NEGATIVE* Interpretation:
> **Conflict Is a *Pain* to Avoid or a *Problem* to Solve**
> → fear, hurt, frustration
>   → *anger*
>   → avoid or attack
>   → *division* and distance & alienation and/or stagnation

The real problem in marriage is not that we have conflict. The root problem is that most of us automatically view conflict as negative rather than something God can use to help us better understand each other. A negative interpretation sees conflict as nothing more than a pain to avoid or a problem to solve. For many, their immediate emotional reaction to conflict is fear, hurt, or frustration, which almost always leads to anger. As we have seen earlier in this chapter, most people deal with their anger by avoiding or attacking their spouse. Either way leads to division and distance in the relationship, which results in alienation and/or stagnation.

As we discussed the different ways people can interpret conflict, Dale and Liz realized that they almost always interpreted it negatively. Dale's pattern was to feel threatened, so he avoided conflict. That's how his dad had done it; that's how Gramps had done it. "How often has this helped to solve the problem?" I asked Dale. "Well," he said, "as I think about it, I don't know that it has ever helped."

Liz's response was the opposite of Dale's. At the point of conflict she would feel hurt and frustrated and so tended to attack. "I just wish Dale would talk about issues for once in his life. Whenever there seems to be an issue, he does his deaf, dumb, and blind act, and then he moves into his disappearing act." What do you think Dale did when he felt attacked? Of course! He withdrew—he sought distance from Liz.

Some of us avoid conflict because we are afraid of being proven wrong. I don't like to be wrong. I mean I *really* don't like to be wrong. Let's face it, nobody enjoys being wrong. Yet there are two ways we can interpret being wrong. If our value, worth, significance, and security are based on our being right all of the time, then being wrong is catastrophic. It means that we're bad, we've failed, we're stupid, we're losers. But we can also see being wrong as an opportunity to learn, grow, change, and become more mature.

What's the price tag for our inability or unwillingness to face problems and learn how to resolve conflicts? It keeps us from knowing ourselves, knowing others, getting close to others, building quality relationships, experiencing meaningful ministry, and experiencing God's best for our lives.

THE GROWTH-FOCUSED (POSITIVE) INTERPRETATION

We can choose to see conflict through God's eyes as a great opportunity for increased growth, maturity, and intimacy. The process of growing into an intimate relationship involves dealing with conflict. Since many of us avoid conflict like the plague, we don't grow, we don't change, we don't get close, and we don't experience any real intimacy. We stay stuck in the rut of shallowness, superficiality, and mediocrity.

In the first few years of our marriage, Carrie and I discovered that rather than deal with the issues, rather than speak the truth in love, it was easier and less threatening to ignore what we were feeling. Short-term that worked. However, over time we discovered the painful reality that eventually the fear, hurt, and frustration became intolerable. At that point one or both of us would dump our frustration on the other one, thus decreasing understanding, safety, and trust and damaging the relationship. Then we would run back to our safe emotional places and start the dance all over again.

If we choose to see conflict from a growth-focused perspective, we are more likely to see it as an opportunity for understanding. This makes it easier for us to risk speaking the truth in love, which leads to an increased sense of safety, trust, and intimacy.

The growth-focused response says:

1. There are personal and relationship issues that are important to me.
2. I care enough about you and our relationship to risk healthy confrontation and speak the truth in love.
3. I don't lose when I'm proven wrong or when I don't get my way, but I *do* lose when I throw away any opportunity to learn, understand, and grow.

Mature people don't avoid, suppress, repress, deny, or ignore conflict. Instead, they train themselves to see it as an opportunity. Once couples come to see the potential of healthy conflict, they are able to exchange their defensive and combative postures for creative ones. They don't feel threatened, they feel challenged. Time and time again we've seen that conflict can be a sovereign opportunity and a divine appointment that God can use to help us "be conformed to the image of His Son" (Romans 8:29 NKJV).

When we choose a positive interpretation of conflict, we actually anticipate what we can learn about each other. Because we know that God can use this conflict, we're more likely to prayerfully consider how we can make a loving confrontation (address the issue) that can lead to the deep levels of intimacy that we both long for.

POSITIVE Interpretation:
Conflict Is an Opportunity to Grow

→ growth-focused anticipation
   → collaboration and *understanding*
      → increased *trust*
         → increased *intimacy*

THE CONFLICT & INTIMACY CYCLE

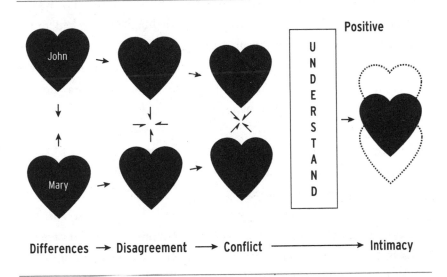

Differences → Disagreement → Conflict → Intimacy

STAGE #5:
Choosing Collaboration and Growth

Now comes what for many is the most difficult part: the challenge of dealing with the disagreements that led to the conflict and choosing to collaborate on solutions. This stage always involves confronting the issues at hand, but unfortunately, as we saw in the last chapter, for many people *confrontation* is a dirty word. However, we're not talking about an in-your-face confrontation of the person, but an open and honest confrontation of the issue.

Confrontation was especially difficult for Dale, who had been a lifelong conflict avoider. Liz had no problem with confronting, but her attack mode always created more heat and hurt than it did light. They decided to try this "growth-focused" approach to dealing with conflict. They flipped a coin to decide who would pick the issue and Liz lost, meaning she also had to practice the healthy confrontation. Liz decided to risk sharing a recurring situation in their relationship that made it hard for her to risk opening up to him. While Liz was as bright as Dale and actually had better verbal skills, Dale had much more formal education and valued a precise use of words. On occasion he would correct Liz in front of their friends when she would use the "wrong" word to express herself. He wasn't even aware that he was doing it, but each time it happened it would reopen a wound of embarrassment and inferiority for Liz.

Before they began the discussion I had them read Romans 12:9–16; 1 Corinthians 13:5–7; Galatians 5:14–15; and Ephesians 4:15–16. Then Dale and Liz began their interaction by praying and asking God to help them better understand each other. Notice their initial goal wasn't to resolve the issue since the majority of marital conflicts are never perfectly resolved. They started out with the very achievable goal of wanting to better understand each other. They agreed that they wanted to balance their personal needs to be understood with their relational need to better understand each other.

As Liz shared her experience of the hurtful situation, Dale listened and asked clarifying questions. He now understood that in these kinds of conversations it was easy for him to feel threatened or criticized, so he intentionally and prayerfully focused on understanding what the situation looked like through Liz's eyes and felt like through her heart. As he chose to focus his attention on understanding his wife he found it a little easier (notice we said a little) not to be defensive.

When Liz finished sharing, Dale asked, "Honey, in the future, how could I respond in ways that might be more honoring to you without my being someone I'm not?" Liz quickly responded, "Wow, I didn't expect you to ask me that. I'm not exactly sure. But I'll pray and think about it and let you know." After a brief pause she squeezed his hand, looked him in the eyes, and said, "Thanks for asking and thanks for listening."

This might seem like a massively insignificant conversation, but it's seemingly *small* conversations like this that help couples like you turn the corner on unhealthy conflict and establish new patterns of growth-focused conflict. In our next time together Dale and Liz shared a couple of other similar discussions they had been able to have on their own. Liz said, "I think we have begun to redefine the role of conflict in our marriage relationship. I never thought I would see that happen."

At the beginning of this chapter we shared the statement of Robert Runcie, Archbishop of Canterbury, to Prince Charles and Lady Diana: "Our faith sees the wedding day not as a place of arrival but the place where the adventure begins." The adventure of becoming one in Christ, of experiencing the deep levels of understanding, safety, trust, and intimacy that God designed to characterize a meaningful *Christian* marriage, involves a healthy, *growth-focused* view of conflict that allows iron to sharpen iron and forge a love that many only dream about, but which God wants to help His children experience as a dream come true.

In this chapter we hope we've helped you turn a corner on your understanding how healthy conflict can actually lead to deeper levels of intimacy. But how can you make it work for you? That's what the next chapter is about.

SMALL BEGINNINGS

1. Do you and your spouse find yourselves caught in the conflict and intimacy cycle?

2. What kind of conflict styles did you see growing up? (Avoid, Attack, Acquiesce, Approach)
3. What is your typical style of dealing with conflict? What is your spouse's style?
4. What keeps you from pursuing healthy conflict with your spouse? What excuses do you use? (I don't want to make waves. It's not worth the hassle. It's not that important.)
5. What's the cost of *not* dealing with conflicts in your marriage?

SEVEN SIMPLE STEPS THROUGH CONFLICT TO INTIMACY

We hope you came away from the last chapter with a whole new understanding of conflict and the fact that healthy conflict can play a vital role in creating intimate marriage relationships. Unfortunately, simply understanding the value of healthy conflict won't help you deal with those nasty conflict issues that seem to pop up at the most unexpected and inopportune times.

You may have finished the last chapter thinking, *Sounds great in theory, but how do we do it?* Okay, we admit that like many things in life, it is easier said than done. But it's also a lot easier than you might think. In this chapter you are going to discover how you can take your new understanding of conflict and actually use it in working though a real issue. What kind of issue should you pick to work on? This point is critical: Whenever you are working on changing deep-seated behavior patterns and learning new skills, it's always important to start with something fairly simple.

It will also be helpful for you to pick something that is primarily your issue and not your spouse's—something that has frustrated, disappointed, discouraged, or bugged you. For the purpose of this chapter, think about a low-ticket, low-priority conflict issue. It should be something you are concerned about but not something that triggers a lot of emotional and relational baggage. At the end of the chapter we've included an outline that you can copy and use in working through this and other conflicts.

As you go through this chapter, remember that these seven steps are merely a suggested starting place. This is one way to do it. Most of the couples we've worked with have taken this and modified it to fit their own unique personalities, relationship, and conflict issues.

BEFORE CONFLICT ARISES

The best place to start dealing with conflict is before a conflict arises. That's right, *before* a conflict arises. Every couple has their own combination of attitudes, emotions, and circumstances that set them up for conflict, but most couples are totally unaware of what they are. As you begin to identify the factors that precede your most frequent conflicts, you will discover a gold mine of insights to help you deal more effectively with those conflicts once they arise. In fact, many couples have told us that this simple process not only helped them clarify and reduce their conflicts but also eliminate many of those silly, unnecessary conflicts that can flare up into a forest fire and ruin an entire evening or weekend.

Start by identifying your frequent conflict issues and determine their seriousness. Many couples find that a majority of their conflicts center around sex, money, parenting, in-laws, leisure time, and holidays. Dale and Liz discovered that over half of their conflicts were in two categories: finances and leisure time.

Next, identify the factors that make you most vulnerable to conflict. Dale found that he was most vulnerable when he had been working too hard and was under pressure to meet some deadline. Busyness and over-commitment increased the probability that he would engage in conflict. Liz realized that she was more vulnerable when the kids had been particularly difficult or when she and Dale hadn't had adequate time together as a couple. If you're not sure what your conflicts center around, ask your spouse, your children, or a friend. They'll be glad to tell you.

Next, ask yourself which of your behaviors might sabotage constructive conflict. For example, does the volume of your voice increase? Do your attacks become more personal? Do you bring up past mistakes and failures, start talking about your spouse's mother, or perhaps exaggerate and say things such as "You always . . ." and "You never . . ." Are you so consumed with communicating your point that you don't make a sincere effort to understand your partner's concerns?

As Dale and Liz answered this question they discovered that both of them had some unhealthy habits that contributed to their failure in resolving conflicts. Liz acknowledged, "My biggest problem behaviors are that I interrupt Dale and at times complete his sentences for him. I have difficulty giving Dale time to think about an issue before discussing it, and I tend to want to solve a problem that we haven't clearly defined." Dale realized, "I need to listen for Liz's heart and not just for the bottom line, and I need to stay with the conversation and not give in to my tendency to withdraw as soon as I get frustrated or uncomfortable."

WHEN CONFLICT ARISES

Regardless of the severity of the conflict, we've found that constructive conflict management is always easier when you have a plan. Over the past twenty years we've worked with hundreds of couples who have told us that the following seven steps have helped them turn conflict from something they feared to an opportunity to increase understanding and intimacy.

STEP #1: DEFINE THE ISSUE. PRAY, LISTEN, AND SEEK UNDERSTANDING

The first step is to acknowledge that there is a problem, set aside ample time to discuss each other's perception of the issue, and work toward an agreed-upon definition. The majority of couples who come for marriage counseling have a history of emotionally painful and relationally damaging conflicts over issues that have never been defined or clarified. For many years we were one of those couples.

Remember this: You will *never* resolve what you don't understand. Human nature dictates that it is virtually impossible to accept advice (let alone criticism) from someone unless you feel that they are trying to understand you. If you want your spouse to understand you, the starting place is for you to take the initiative in understanding them. Answering the following questions will help you better understand and define the issue.

Whose issue is it?

Usually one person has more invested in a particular issue than their spouse. Is this an issue that one of you feels more strongly about than the other? Where did those strong opinions and feelings come from? Is it a recent or a long-standing issue?

What kind of issue is it?

Conflict comes in all shapes and sizes. Some issues are interpersonal, some relate to ideas and opinions, and others relate to fairly low-level daily concerns.

Is there more than one issue involved?

Most people (including Carrie and me) have spent hours engaged in conflicts that involved several issues. It's hard enough to manage one issue. It's almost impossible to deal with several issues at the same time. If there is more than one issue, decide which is most urgent. Which is most important? What order should we take them in? If you can't agree, then choose the least volatile issue first. If you can't agree on that, then just flip a coin. Yes, that may sound silly, but we've been flipping coins for years and it works.

What is my spouse's core concern?

A critical part of defining an issue is to take time to understand the heart and the perspective of your spouse. In fact, this may be one of the greatest contributions healthy conflict makes to the growth of intimacy in a marriage. The Bible has a lot to say about the power of seeking understanding. Proverbs 4:7 says, "Though it cost all you have, get *understanding*" (emphasis added).

Listening is one of the most powerful intimacy builders in any relationship because listening leads to understanding. That's why James exhorts us to "be quick to listen, slow to speak" (1:19). When you choose to listen to another person, you are saying that you value them and their concerns and that they are worth taking the time to understand. An open ear is the sure sign of an open heart.

Listening sounds like a simple thing, but the tragic truth is that most of us aren't good listeners. Studies have shown that most people can listen five times as fast as someone else can speak. This means that during a conversation, especially one involving conflict, it's easy for your mind to wander to what you're going to say and how you are going to defend yourself when the other person stops speaking.

We don't understand that there is a big difference between hearing and listening. Hearing happens, but listening is a choice. It is a choice to focus on what the other person is saying and try to understand what they really mean. Listening is a form of love, it is a gift, and it is essential to achieving the levels of understanding that will lead to true intimacy.

Notice, we're not asking you to agree with your spouse. We're only suggesting that you invest a few minutes to try to *see* things through their eyes, to *hear* things through their ears, and to *feel* things with their heart. Put yourself in their shoes and see what the issue looks like. We've had many couples tell us that at the end of this exercise they realized that what they had thought was a major problem was nothing more than a misunderstanding, and they didn't need to go any further in the process, thus saving themselves a lot of unnecessary pain and wasted time and energy.

What is my core concern?

After you've chosen to listen, hear, and understand your spouse, it will be important for you to identify and clarify your core concern. Is it only one or are there several of them?

Dale and Liz made the wise decision to start with a fairly safe conflict. They agreed to work on their frustrating differences in estimating time. They narrowed it down even further to the times when they were together and Liz wanted to make a "quick" stop to pick up something.

"One of the conflicts Liz and I had for years had to do with our different sense of timing, especially when it came to her shopping," Dale said. At this point in their marriage, Dale realized their personality differences were a key part of this conflict. "I'm structured, precise, and organized. I probably glance at my wrist every ten minutes to check the time, whether I need to or not. Liz is a sort of spontaneous, free-spirited person who owns a watch but isn't sure why."

Sometimes when they were out shopping, they would come to a store and Liz would tell Dale, "I need to run in here for something." Dale would ask, "How long will you be?" and she would give him her usual answer: "Oh, no more than fifteen minutes."

In Dale's mind that's what it meant, exactly fifteen minutes. In Liz's mind it could mean up to an hour! When the fifteen minutes was up Dale would begin to get frustrated, and it didn't take long for his primary emotion of frustration to turn into the secondary emotion of anger. Finally, when she did return, his unhealthy anger would take over and they would get into it. He accused her of being inconsiderate and thoughtless, and she accused him of being rigid and inflexible.

Once you define the problem, and before going any further, commit this specific conflict—as well as your desire to deal with conflict in a healthier and more mature manner—to God in prayer. In 1 Thessalonians 5:17, we're encouraged to "pray without ceasing" (NKJV). We'll come back to the value and relational power of prayer when we look at Step #7.

In her practical book *The Dance of Anger,* Dr. Harriet Lerner lists twelve Do's and Don'ts of dealing with conflict:

1. Do speak up when an issue is important to you.
2. Don't strike while the iron is hot.
3. Do take time to think about the problem and to clarify your position.
4. Don't use "below-the-belt" tactics.
5. Do speak in "I" language.
6. Don't make vague requests.
7. Do try to appreciate the fact that people are different.
8. Don't participate in intellectual arguments that go nowhere.
9. Do recognize that each person is responsible for his/her own behavior.
10. Don't tell another person what he or she thinks or feels or "should" think or feel.
11. Do try to avoid speaking through a third party.
12. Don't expect change to come from hit-and-run confrontations.

STEP #2: HOW IMPORTANT IS IT? IS IT A HIGH-TICKET OR A LOW-TICKET ITEM?

Once you have defined the issue, the next step is to determine just how important it is. Many of the conflicts in marriage can be traced to personal idiosyncrasies, minor annoyances, or passing irritations.

Researchers tell us that only 31 percent of a couple's major continuing disagreements are about issues that they will be able to resolve. The rest, 69 percent, are about irresolvable perpetual problems—that is, fundamental differences in personalities or basic needs—that will never get resolved but that we need to learn how to manage and deal with.

Some differences demand confrontation, while others are simply a part of living with someone else. We all have our frustrating annoyances and idiosyncrasies and so do our spouses. It's just that ours seem so much less weird, unusual, and even bizarre than theirs.

Before you allow an issue to consume too much of your time, ask yourself, "How important is this?" Is it a high-ticket or a low-ticket item? On a scale of one to ten, a low-ticket item would score only a one through a five. A low-ticket item is something that may irritate or frustrate you, but on the Richter Scale of relationships it really isn't that big a deal. Squeezing the toothpaste in at the wrong end or not loading the dishwasher the way you'd like it to be loaded are low-ticket issues.

A high-ticket item would rate a six through a ten. High-ticket items would include issues such as how affection is expressed, how important decisions are made, who decides where we spend our vacations, how finances are allocated, where we live.

High levels of emotion don't mean that it's a high-ticket issue, and low levels of emotion don't mean it's a low-ticket issue. When people have strong emotions about an issue they assume that it's high-ticket, but in fact it may be something fairly insignificant.

This next point is critical. Just because an issue is low-ticket to you doesn't mean it will be low-ticket to your spouse. If you don't treat what your spouse perceives to be a high-ticket issue as high-ticket, then you are discounting them and their reality.

For Liz the time issue was low-ticket. She didn't have a problem when Dale took more time than he thought he would and didn't understand why it seemed such a problem for him when she took longer. While she rated the issue a two, Liz was surprised to hear that Dale gave it a five. "When I first became aware of her tendency to do this I would have given it a one or a two," Dale said, "but since it happens so frequently, even when I've told her it bugs me, it has become even more frustrating and irritating. In fact, at times it feels like a seven or an eight." While this didn't make sense to Liz, she realized that it was something worth dealing with.

STEP #3: ASK YOURSELF: "WHAT IS MY CONTRIBUTION TO THE PROBLEM?"

It's amazing that whenever there is a conflict we usually have little difficulty identifying our spouse's contribution to the problem, but we can be substantially blinded to our own. It's fascinating how very clear many of us can be about how "they" need to change, what "they" could do differently, and how "they" could listen better.

It's easy for us to pray, "Lord, please change them. Please help them see things as clearly as I do. Please give them the same wisdom and insight you've given me." For over ten years I served on the board of directors and national speaking team for Promise Keepers, and I would somewhat jokingly tell the men, "It's easy for men to pray, 'Change my *wife*, O Lord' rather than, in the words of a popular praise song, 'Change my *life*, O Lord.'"

Proverbs 25:12 (TLB) tells us, "It is a badge of honor to accept valid criticism." Those are sound words. Listen to what the other person has to say. Even if 90 percent of what they are saying is invalid, look for the 10 percent that might be true. Look for even the 1 percent that God could use in your life to help you deepen and mature into a more Christlike woman or man.

Sometimes we may just have a difference of opinion. Sometimes there may be sin that God wants us to deal with. I (Gary) have discovered that identifying and taking responsibility for my own sinfulness has helped me see how much I am like everyone else: broken, longing for love, prone to blame, yearning to be understood, self-deceived, desperate for mercy and a grace that is greater than all my sin. Once we see the sin in our own lives we are free to enjoy God's grace and no longer have to fake it or worry about others finding out that we are nothing more than redeemed ragamuffins.

Dale and Liz both acknowledged their contribution to their conflict over shopping. Liz realized that what often caused her to take longer than she thought was that, once in the store, she saw some other things she forgot she needed and decided to go ahead and pick them up. This often took more time than she thought. Dale realized that he was much more rigid than he needed to be. When some of his stops took more time, Liz never made a big deal about it. But whenever she took more time, he always mentioned it.

STEP #4: DO I NEED TO APOLOGIZE OR ASK FOR FORGIVENESS?

As you think and pray through the third step you may become aware of something you have done that you need to apologize or ask forgiveness for. Early in our marriage I learned that I could be right, but go about being right in a wrong or an unhealthy way. In the intensity of an emotional discussion it's easy to say things or do things or express ourselves in a tone of voice that discounts and wounds our partner. Over the next few years I discovered that there were some things I needed to apologize for. My intentions had been good, but my words had wounded the person I loved the most. When I realized how thoughtless and unkind I had been, it was easy for me to apologize and ask Carrie to forgive me. This area of forgiveness is so critical to the development of intimacy that all of chapter 11 is devoted to it.

Since Liz didn't think she had done anything wrong she didn't see any reason to ask for forgiveness. However, as she listened to Dale she realized that there had been numerous occasions when her taking more time than he had allowed for had caused him to be late for or even miss another commitment. With weariness and frustration in his voice, Dale turned to Liz and said, "There are times when an errand you say will take only fifteen minutes ends up taking over an hour and it's not a problem. But there are other times when it really puts me behind, makes me late for something, and makes me look irresponsible. I don't like that." Dale went on to say that what Liz saw as unhealthy anger was really the primary emotion of frustration. He had never actually identified it or tried to express it in a mature and healthy way. As Liz better understood how her choices were impacting Dale in a negative way she realized her need to both apologize and ask for forgiveness.

STEP #5: CHOOSE RADICAL RESPONSIBILITY

Radical responsibility is our way of saying that we need to take personal responsibility to choose what we can do differently and not wait around for our spouse to do something different. It means that we make a unilateral decision, regardless of what our spouse chooses to say or do, to seek wisdom and understanding in dealing with conflict.

Regardless of the habits you saw growing up and those that may have characterized you for most of your life, you can teach yourself to take radical responsibility to listen, to understand, to accept, to be kind, to be patient, to forgive, and to love even when your partner may not be making that same choice. In fact, we are most like our Lord Jesus Christ when we love in this kind of situation.

Radical responsibility can involve cultivating the "power of the compliment." Practice complimenting your spouse. Practice catching them being healthy, scanning for the sovereign presence in their life. Research shows that the most effective way to modify someone's behavior—to get them to do more or less of something—is to reinforce or positively reward that person when that individual is doing what we want them to do. In other words, catch your spouse in the act of getting it right and bring on the fanfare! A well-timed compliment, hug, or note of appreciation goes a lot further than a heart-to-heart about marital dissatisfaction.

When Dale and Liz looked at Step #5, Dale immediately responded: "Over the years I've fussed and stewed and been frustrated by your being late, and the only times I've said something it's been negative, critical, and unkind. What I've said has usually come out of an unhealthy anger. I've never really tried to help you understand how your behavior was a problem for me. I've also never thanked you for the many times that you've kept your word as to the time it would take." That's a great illustration of radical responsibility. He didn't wait for Liz to say something. He took responsibility for what he could do better.

By the time you've gone through the first five steps, you may have no more need to go on to Step #6. Often couples discover that what they thought was a big problem was nothing more than a minor irritation or miscommunication that has disappeared. But if you do need to continue, you will be in a much better place to take the next step.

STEP #6: CHOOSE WHAT YOU BOTH CAN DO DIFFERENTLY

At this point you are working on identifying a mutually acceptable solution. Ah, this sounds so easy. Over time it can become easy, but in the early stages of changing your deep-seated conflict patterns it may be rather difficult. Through our seminars and workshops we discovered that it was much easier for us to help other couples work through these steps than it was to work through them ourselves. Actually it was very embarrassing for us when we came to this realization. Don't be upset or disappointed. Don't give up. It's normal! You are normal!

When it comes to Step #6, be sure to set aside ample time for discussion and prayer. Find a quiet place with no interruptions. Take the phone off the hook. Remember that this step involves choosing to bargain some of your personal needs for some of your relationship needs. Many couples have found it helpful to read 1 Corinthians 13 aloud before entering into the discussion.

In our seminars we've had people raise their hands and ask, "But what if we can't agree on a mutually acceptable solution?" After a brief pause one of us usually smiles and responds by saying, "Well, if you can't agree on a solution, reach into your pocket, pull out a coin, ask the other person if they want heads or tails, and flip it." This usually brings a lot of laughter, but we're quick to tell them that we are serious. As we said earlier, we've become professional coin flippers. Hey, it's better to try something that might work than to continue doing something that is a proven failure. Remember that "crazy" is to find out what doesn't work and then to keep on doing it.

If you've had a similar issue that you were able to resolve, how did you do it? What did you do or say that allowed you to either resolve or live with the difference in a way that was acceptable?

If you've never been able to manage or resolve a similar issue, make a list of what you've tried that hasn't worked. Then make a list of what you haven't tried. You may find it helpful to talk to some other individuals or couples who have been in similar situations. What worked for them? What did they learn as they worked through their conflict? Be careful not to ignore a potential solution just because you don't think it will work. Get as many ideas as possible on your list. Look them over. Talk about them. You may find that pieces of two or three different ideas come together to provide a solution neither one of you had considered. If the first solution you try doesn't work, then move on to the next option. It may take three or four attempts before you find something that works. Couples who follow through with these suggestions find that over time there are very few issues they can't deal with.

In Step #6, list the specific steps involved and who is responsible to do what. This is an important part that most people leave out. What are the specific steps involved in the solution? Who is going to do what? When will they do it? For how long will they do it? When will you let each other know that you have done what you agreed to do? If your issue is finances, who is going to record the checks, and when will you meet each month to check your progress? If the issue is child care, who will be responsible to check out the different options? Who will make the calls, and when will you do it?

Dale and Liz made a list of seven changes they would be willing to make:

1. If Liz wants to make a quick stop, she will only pick up what she said she was going in for and nothing else.
2. Liz can make her estimate and then add an additional five minutes as a buffer. If the errand takes a little longer than expected, no problem. If she comes back earlier, that's all the better.
3. Dale can offer to go into the store to pick up the item.
4. Dale can "mellow out" about Liz being exact in her estimate of how long an errand might take. If she is within ten minutes,

that will be considered the same as being on time.

5. If it takes more time than Liz thought, she will let Dale know why.

6. If Dale has a time crunch to get to another commitment, he will let Liz know. If he doesn't, he can bring a book to read since that's one of his favorite things to do.

7. They can do the errand together.

STEP #7: PRAY ABOUT IT, DO IT, AND REVIEW IT!

Pray About It

The first part of Step #7 is so obvious, but it took us years to learn it. There is an enormous relational value to prayer that we didn't begin to discover until we were about ten years into our marriage. Oh, we knew that prayer was important. We knew all the passages and promises on prayer. We had read books on prayer together, and we talked to others about the importance of prayer, but we didn't really pray together, especially during times of conflict. What we probably needed to do the most during our conflicts was something we tended to do the least, if at all.

Over the years God showed us something that actually transformed the way we deal with conflict and transformed our marriage. We discovered there are several relational nutrients to prayer that are unbelievably powerful intimacy builders.

Relational nutrient #1 is that prayer produces an increased *perspective* of each other's heart. When I hear Carrie pray, I hear a side of her heart that I often miss in the heat of a conflict. I hear her love for the Lord, her love for me, and her desire to be a godly wife and friend to me. I hear her hurts, discouragement, disappointment, and frustration through a different set of ears. It's amazing how simply hearing my wife pray can open up my heart to her and to the Lord and change a combative heart into a collaborative heart.

Relational nutrient #2 is that prayer produces increased *power* for our relationships. When I hear Gary pray, I'm reminded that in the big scheme of things the issue probably isn't as earth-shattering as I thought. I'm reminded that God is more concerned about our experiencing love and intimacy than we are. I'm reminded that while I may feel drained, He has promised to supply all of my needs and I can trust Him to be a promise keeper. Prayer often empowers me not to give in or give up.

Relational nutrient #3 is that prayer produces increased *passion* for God and one another. When we spend time in prayer, we discover that God gives us a bit more of His mind and His heart for us and for our situation. We understand that the most important result of the conflict may not be the solution but how we choose to honor, love, and respect each other in the process of dealing with the conflict. The more we focus on God's love for us and His promise to help us love each other with His love, the more we actually find ourselves wanting to understand, listen to, and work with each other. On many occasions prayer has dissolved or significantly weakened the stone walls we had erected between us. In prayer God infuses our hearts with a perspective, a power, and a passion that only He can give us. The more of Christ we see in each other's lives, the more attractive we become to each other and the more Christlike we want to be.

So what does praying together actually look like? It can be as simple as joining hands and spending sixty seconds in silent prayer. It can involve each partner praying aloud for one or two minutes and then when finished, squeezing the hand of the other so they can pray. When we started to pray during conflicts we didn't take a lot of time. Even a little bit of time was helpful. Now, sixteen years later, we will sometimes spend much more time. However, the important thing is not how much time you spend, but that you do it! Our friends Dave and Jan Stoop have written a wonderful little book, *When Couples Pray,* that is packed with simple and practical suggestions to strengthen any couple's prayer life.

Although they had rarely prayed together as a couple, Dale and Liz found this step to be the easiest one. They were so tired of doing the same old dysfunctional dance over and over again, of rooting around in the same old relational rut, that they embraced the real hope they had discovered in this simple seven-step process. "Actually," Liz said, "by the time we finished our list in Step #6, the hardest part was over. All we had to do was pray about it and then do it."

Do It!

You've run from it, hid from it, fought about it, and cried over it, and now you have the opportunity to do it. It may be one of those issues you can resolve or one of those perpetual issues you need to figure out how to live with. You have defined the problem, considered your contribution to it, discussed possible solutions, agreed on where to start, and clarified who will do what. Now's your chance to make it work—or to find out it doesn't work. Either way, you both win. You are one step closer to discovering what will work to resolve or better manage the conflict, and in the process you've listened to, loved, and honored each other.

Don't wait for the best time. Put your plan into action now. Failure isn't trying something and finding it doesn't work on the first try. Failure is continuing to stay stuck in the rut of what hasn't worked in the past and probably won't in the future.

Review It!

When you've given your plan adequate time, it's important to get together and discuss the results. How well has this solution worked? Were there any surprises? How could we improve it? How did I change? How did my partner change? What did I learn about myself from this conflict? What did I learn about our relationship? What did I learn about God's faithfulness? What did I learn about what I can do differently next time?

For years Dale and Liz had experienced frustrating and futile fights over the same issue. Not only did they resolve this issue, but through the process they grew in their understanding and appreciation for each other's differences. "We're still very different in how we view time," Liz said as she reached out to take Dale's hand, "but now we understand each other better and are able to give more grace to each other." "Was there one part of the process that was especially helpful?" I (Gary) asked. As we talked through each step they realized that for them each step was invaluable.

As they learned how to define the problem they were able to clarify and agree on what they wanted to work on. They weren't trying to fix five issues, just one. They were wise in starting with a comparatively low-ticket issue, but since it was something that had at times caused some significant frustration for Dale, he especially wanted to address it. "I think that Step #3 helped me turn a real corner in how I understood the problem," Dale said. "At first I thought it was all Liz's problem and that she was the one who needed to change, but in Step #3, I realized there were some things that I could do a better job at.

"When we finished Step #6, it was easy for us to take the final step." By the end of the process they saw the problem, themselves, and each other from a new perspective. Their understanding led to a greater sense of safety and security, which over time deepened their sense of trust and intimacy. Not only were they successful in resolving a long-standing issue, they had learned new ways to deal with anger and had learned the value of healthy conflict. Dale said, "I discovered that underneath the anger I had dumped on Liz was the primary emotion of frustration." As he expressed his frustration with Liz's being late she was able to hear him, understand what the situation looked like through his eyes, and respond in ways that honored his concerns.

Dale continued, "So now when Liz says she's going shopping, I ask, 'Do you have a rough approximation of when you might be through?' Liz smiles and says, 'Oh, in about an hour or two.' This humorous response takes the pressure off both of us. We now have a plan. If I go with her, I can take a book to read. If I only have a half hour, I let her know. And often she's back much sooner than she used to be." After a brief pause he concluded, "Maybe we've both changed."

SEVEN SIMPLE STEPS THROUGH HEALTHY CONFLICT TO INTIMACY

Step 1: Define the issue. Pray, listen, and seek understanding.
- •• Whose issue is it?
- •• What kind of issue is it?
- •• Is there more than one issue involved?
- •• What is my spouse's core concern?
- •• What is my core concern?

Step 2: How important is it? Is it a high-ticket or a low-ticket item?

Step 3: Ask yourself, "What is my contribution to the problem?"

Step 4: Do I need to apologize or ask for forgiveness?

Step 5: Choose radical responsibility.

Step 6: Choose what you both can do differently.

Step 7: Pray about it, do it, and review it!

FORGIVENESS: THE HEALING OIL OF INTIMACY

Make allowance for each other's faults, and forgive anyone who offends you. Remember, the Lord forgave you, so you must forgive others. (Colossians 3:13 NLT*)*

Our hope for this book has been to help you work through anger so that you can experience the intimacy that God designed for you to enjoy with Him and with each other. The goal of intimacy is to bond, to connect, to knit two hearts together in love. One of the key components of intimacy that we discussed in chapter 2 is the ability to forgive and to ask for forgiveness. Forgiveness is essential in order for any relationship to keep growing and for trust to deepen or be reestablished if broken. Forgiveness is the avenue, the path that we must walk down if we are to let go of anger, resentment, and negativity toward our spouse, which almost always hinders intimacy.

Because forgiveness can be misunderstood and is not practiced well, a chapter is not too much to devote to this very important biblical discipline. Forgiveness has a powerful influence on the levels of trust and intimacy a couple experiences. When trust is broken we feel insecure. Having a good understanding and experience of forgiveness greatly affects our security level in a relationship. Think about it. How secure do we feel when we doubt that God has forgiven us or that He could forgive us?

For many, coming to Christ is the first real awareness of the need for forgiveness. We come to believe that Jesus Christ truly died for *our* sin. We may picture our sin as the worst, or we may think we are okay (really we have not done anything too bad). "There are many who have done so much more than I have sin-wise," we tell ourselves. We can carry this mentality into our marriage and hurt the level of trust our spouse has in us if we are unwilling to take responsibility for even the smallest wrongs toward our beloved.

Forgiveness is the healing balm that keeps a relationship vibrant and growing. Forgiveness propels us forward. A lack of forgiveness often keeps us wounded and stuck in the past. In fact, if you notice in your marriage that the past is brought up frequently, there is probably a lack of true forgiveness. Wounds held inside fester, will eventually come to the surface, and almost always threaten intimacy. Forgiveness is the pathway to freedom, peace, and a deepened trust. Unforgiveness leads us down the pathway of destructive anger, leading to built-up resentment. We see our spouse through the eyes of our wounds and not much else. Here are some ways in which wounds may come into play in our marriage.

WOUNDS COME IN ALL DIFFERENT SIZES AND SHAPES

Early on in her marriage to Tom, Lisa began to feel some hurts building up. Being on time was important to Lisa, and when she said she would be someplace at a certain time, that is exactly what she meant. Consequently, she expected others to function the same way.

Tom approached things differently. When Tom said 6:30, that could mean 6:45 or even 7:00, but it rarely meant 6:30. Lisa assumed that Tom was disregarding her perspective about time. She felt his lateness communicated the message that what he wanted and what he decided were more important than what she wanted and decided. While this wound may seem small to some, it began to build in Lisa, causing her to question Tom's trustworthiness and his sensitivity to her needs. She felt angry and betrayed.

Jack felt that Beth's dad did not always respect him. His father-in-law criticized Jack's mechanical ability or lack thereof, his job, and his parenting. What hurt Jack is that Beth did not seem to stick up for him. Beth seemed to ignore what her dad would say, leaving Jack very insecure about her view of him. Jack began to believe that Beth loved her dad more, that her dad's view of Jack was right, and that he needed to change. He felt wounded, angry, and betrayed.

After fifteen years of marriage, Heather and Greg found themselves dealing with what many couples feel is the ultimate betrayal—an affair. It began slowly as a friendship at work. Heather went back to work part time after staying home with their children in the early years of their childhood. She met a man in her department who was charming, communicative, and fun. At first they did things together with other co-workers, but with time began to talk on their cell phones and e-mail one another. As is often the case, the emotional affair transitioned into a sexual affair. Greg was feeling uneasy about his marriage and began to go searching for what he feared most. He read Heather's e-mail and looked at her cell phone bill and found out about her interaction with this other man. Anger, hurt, and betrayal left him with deep wounds.

Wounds can occur in all sorts of circumstances. For example, you may need your spouse to share in a traumatic doctor's appointment,

173

but they choose not to join you. Your spouse does not share in household jobs, even when you have asked them to. Your spouse leaves you on the weekend to do their activities without discussing it with you (or even after discussing it still chooses to do these activities more frequently than you would like). Your spouse does not see your need for romance and dating. Your spouse uses the word *divorce* during a conflict; or your spouse calls you a name.

Anger and resentment may keep reentering the relationship if these wounds have not been resolved through the process of forgiveness and restoration. Many of us have experienced this and understand what it feels like. The seemingly small wounds that I have not truly asked forgiveness for or continue to inflict keep playing into much of how Gary and I interact. I have hurt him by not being a good listener. If I am not a good listener and I don't see the need to change this about myself, how can he trust me to listen when he hurts, when he has an idea, or when there is a conflict? If I have not changed my behavior, his response to me will not be one related to the moment, but more likely be related to wounds that have not been resolved. The same is true in the marriages we have cited above.

Tom's lack of punctuality leaves Lisa feeling disregarded, and she carries her feelings into other realms of their relationship. She may feel he disregards her as a person, especially when she is vulnerable and hurt. Jack feels like a failure in his wife's eyes because he doesn't meet Beth's dad's expectations. When an affair has not been healed through the process of forgiveness and restoration, this deep wound can keep cropping up for the duration of a marriage. Without acknowledgment, forgiveness, and restoration the marriage may not survive.

WHAT IS FORGIVENESS?

In our research for this book, in our work with couples and individuals, in our study of Scripture, and in our own marriage we've found that forgiveness is not always easy. People have a difficult time going through the process of forgiveness. Yet forgiveness is required by God. In the Lord's Prayer (Matthew 6:12) we ask forgiveness to the degree we have forgiven others. Matthew 18:35 says that our heavenly Father will treat us according to how we have treated others. We are to be kind and compassionate to one another, forgiving each other, just as God through Christ has forgiven us (Ephesians 4:32).

Webster's defines *forgive* in this way: "to cease to feel resentment against . . . to give up resentment of or claim to requital for an insult." When we forgive, we give up our perceived right to hold on to the wrong, wound, or debt that someone has caused us. When we forgive, we no longer bring the past into the present. When God forgives, He tosses our sins as far away as the east is from the west. Not so easy with us humans! We want to hold on to our hurt; we want to make the other person pay because somehow we believe it will make us feel better. We believe the person who caused our hurt deserves our punishment.

The problem is that we are the losers! We are the ones left with the bitterness, insecurity, and lack of trust that invade other areas of our life, including intimacy with our spouse. Anger, obsession, anxiety, and depression can result from our choice not to forgive. Forgiveness releases us from bondage.

Forgiveness involves every one of us. We will all at some time need to forgive someone for hurting us, and we will all need the forgiveness of another for hurting them. This is why the process and practice of forgiveness is so vital to the health and intimacy of marriage. Because we are still sinners as long as we are living on this earth, we will make mistakes by hurting each other, both intentionally and unintentionally.

It is vital that we work to change our sinful behavior. To blatantly continue to do things that hurt our spouse is not consistent with repentance and restoration. Early in our marriage I was good at saying I was "sorry" to Gary. I wanted to get beyond the conflict and move on to being close again. The problem with this approach is that I may have felt somewhat sorry for my behavior, but what was most important to me was that I would feel better. I was less concerned that I had hurt Gary and that I needed to stop doing these things that hurt him. I needed to repent of my actions and demonstrate to him, over time, that I was actively changing the hurtful behavior. Changing the behavior helps to restore the trust, safety, and intimacy of the relationship. Often we take our spouse for granted and "blow off" the things we need to change about ourselves in order to deepen their trust. I do this when I say I am going to do something Gary asks me to do and then I don't do it. He learns he cannot trust me to follow through. In order for intimacy to grow, the process of forgiveness has to incorporate true repentance and an effort to change our behavior.

WHAT FORGIVENESS IS NOT

We don't necessarily forget the wrong after we have forgiven it. The memories may crop up out of nowhere, but with time our emotions do not take over as they did before. Remembering something that hurt does not mean that we are still wounded or that the wound is invading our lives and our relationships. Even though we still feel pain, that doesn't mean that we have not forgiven. I still feel pain from something Gary said a long time ago. I do not feel the pain every time I remember the event and I am not obsessed with the event like I used to be, but at times I do feel pain. I use that opportunity to thank God for His forgiveness of me. I thank Him for helping me to forgive Gary, and I thank Him that Gary has forgiven me for not always being what he has needed. This helps with the hurt and keeps me from allowing the pain to take over.

Another way to let go of the pain is to focus on the precious aspects of our spouse. Yes, our spouse will hurt us and we will hurt them, but if we have gone through the process of forgiveness, repentance, and restoration, we have the opportunity to remember what is precious to us about our spouse. It is good to practice thinking on the lovely things concerning Gary: his gifts, his talents, his love for me, and the fact that he is a great dad. It is much easier to remember what is not helpful. It seems that thinking on the negative and the hurtful comes so much easier! No wonder we are exhorted to take captive every thought (2 Corinthians 10:5) and to think on whatever is pure and lovely (Philippians 4:8).

By forgiving someone, we are not saying they have not hurt us or they have not done anything wrong. It simply releases them from the debt, and it releases us from the anger and bitterness.

HOW TO WORK THROUGH FORGIVENESS

Marsha and Bill had not practiced the art of forgiving in their marriage to the extent that they could feel the benefits and the impact of forgiveness on their level of intimacy and trust. The little things that can wound were piling up in their hearts. They would get along okay until there was conflict, and then these wounds would come pouring out of them. Rarely could they resolve a conflict because of the deep anger, hurt, and resentment from the years of built-up wounds. With the help of a counselor, Marsha and Bill began to see that they both needed to forgive and be forgiven.

Forgiveness often involves being able to see our own fallen state and to see that we are people who are capable of causing hurt in someone else. As simple as this may sound, many of us do not want to accept the fact that we can hurt others! Often we are too busy focusing on our own hurts. Marsha and Bill began to go back and talk through their wounds one at a time.

Before we embark on forgiving, we may need to take a good look at ourselves and see what is bottled up inside. We need to see what we have not forgiven, to see our hurt and acknowledge our anger. In some cases we may need to take our wounds to God, crawl onto His lap, and let Him soothe us. If our spouse has betrayed us through an affair or the use of pornography, we may need to feel these offenses to the fullest before there is any change. God sometimes allows us to be in great need before He begins to heal us. It may be only at this point that we are ready to begin the process of forgiveness.

Talk about the issue: It is much more effective if a couple can stick to one offense at a time! Talk about the issue or the event that caused the wound.

Share emotions: It is important to put into words the pain and emotions that have been associated with an issue or event. This conversation may happen more than one time depending on the event. In the case of an affair, it is a process that may take a year to work through, whereas in the case of being late, it may take only a couple of times to talk out the wound. The important thing here is that emotions are put into words and the person needing the forgiveness understands what they have done and how their spouse feels.

Ask for forgiveness: Only after discussion and understanding does the offender ask for forgiveness. The person who has been offended may be ready to forgive at this point or they may need some time. Time does not mean using the pain to beat up the offender, but rather to take in the words of your spouse and at least begin to believe them at a cognitive level. Dr. Everett Worthington explains his theory of decisional forgiveness and emotional forgiveness. Decisional forgiveness is something we choose to give, but emotional forgiveness may take quite some time to catch up with us.[1] Forgiveness is a process, not a one-time event. This is precisely why we need to practice forgiveness in marriage—so wounds do not build up over time.

The offender may take steps to redeem the behavior: This is what we hope will happen in our marriage. The chronically late spouse may get better, but not completely to the point we would like to see. We want our spouse to stick up for us with our in-laws, but in reality they may not always do this either. I try to listen better to Gary, but at times I still miss all that he's saying. I have prayed about this and asked God to help me see when I am not listening. I've asked God to help me go to Gary and tell him I could have listened to him better, but I'm still working on this in my life. In order to change we have to understand that only God can change us. We have the opportunity to embrace our dependence on Him. We can also check in with our spouse to see how we are doing. That's a pretty vulnerable place to put yourself in! But it's worth the level of intimacy it can reap.

WHEN YOUR SPOUSE DOES NOT SEE THEIR WRONG

In any relationship, including our relationship with the Lord, we are sometimes blinded to our wrong behavior and our need for forgiveness. In most marriages there will be instances where you will feel like you need to forgive your spouse for hurting you. You may bring up the issue, but they simply do not see that they have done anything to hurt you or that they need to change something about themselves.

The good news is that we have the power of the Lord Jesus Christ at work in our relationship. We also have the power of prayer. If your spouse does not immediately acknowledge a wrong, instead of pounding them with your hurt, you might simply let them know that you still have some hurt with regard to an issue and that you hope they will be open to looking at themselves and pray about it as well. Continue on your own to ask God to help you forgive your spouse for what they have done.

Maybe your spouse will never be good at being on time or taking the trash out or doing some other task. There may be some things you can let go of and live with. Certainly we are not talking about letting a spouse continue to have sexual affairs or to involve themselves in pornography. But there are lower-ticket items that you can forgive and leave behind.

You can pray that God will be at work in your spouse to soften their heart toward yours. Ask God to continue to show you what you need to change in order to wound your spouse less and love them more. The forgiveness process is a challenge. It is so challenging that we needed a Savior to die on a cross for our sinful behavior so that we might be forgiven. No wonder we will need to be at work in our relationships on this earth to incorporate forgiveness into our hearts and into practice in order to experience greater intimacy!

BEYOND FORGIVENESS

Yes, forgiveness can be a healing oil to a relationship and a balm to restore the trust we long for in our marriage. Sometimes, depending on the offense and the level to which the offender wants to change, trust may take some time to build again. Remember that trust does not come naturally to most of us. Because of the fall we are not very good at trusting. Many of us find it difficult to trust that Jesus loves us, let alone our spouse. Trust involves assuming the best about our spouse and that they desire to show their love for us in meaningful ways. We may also need to look at ourselves and improve on ways we can be trusted.

Trust involves grace. Grace means we acknowledge that our spouse isn't perfect, we are not perfect, and neither one of us will achieve perfection on earth. Grace means we love unconditionally. We choose to trust that God is working in our spouse to be the person He created them to be. As I trust Gary's love and care for me I can forgive him his failures toward me because I know that he will never be perfect on this earth. He will hurt me, sometimes intentionally and sometimes unintentionally. What I desire is to be committed to forgiving him and allowing God to continue to show me my weaknesses and where I can become someone Gary can trust even deeper with time.

A key ingredient for successful and long-term restoration and deepened intimacy is empathy. Webster's defines *empathy* as "the capacity for participation in another's feelings or ideas." In order to love well we must develop and practice this ability to get behind the eyes of another and see their world at least in a measure the way they see it. If I don't have empathy for you, if I don't try to see things the way you see them, then I will not know your heart and you will not know mine. Empathy gets me looking at you and your heart when I would tend to only want you to see my heart. When I see your heart I am acting on Ephesians 4:32. I can't be compassionate toward you if I don't try to see your world from your heart.

The morning Gary shared that he was hurt when Nathan didn't listen to his experience and fatherly advice (which we discussed in chapter 3), I had a choice. I could get into his heart at that moment, feel some of his feelings, and be tenderhearted toward him, but I chose to let Gary know he was wrong for feeling that way. I wounded him. I told him that his feelings didn't count. If I had been practicing empathy, I would have felt his feelings at some level and I would have acknowledged that they counted. We need empathy to love and to forgive. When I see your world through your eyes, I don't blame you so much for getting it wrong sometimes. I hurt for you, I desire to be gentle with you, and I am more apt to forgive you.

Forgiveness is essential for intimacy. God knew that when He set this system up to right wrongs and express hurts. Forgiveness is essential for any relationship to grow and thrive. To forgive a wrong releases your spouse from the prison you've kept them in. It also releases you from the prison you've built for yourself out of bitterness, anger, resentment—a laundry list of wrongs not dealt with, and so much more.

It is difficult for a marriage to sustain a continued lack of forgiveness. Not being able to ask for forgiveness or to forgive contributes to negativity, undermines the practice of assuming the best about your spouse, keeps us from a heart that longs to understand our spouse, and prevents intimacy. Forgiveness is such a powerful component to marriage that without it the relationship begins to atrophy. Forgiveness strengthens the heart's ability to connect and stay connected just like weight lifting strengthens muscles.

If this part of your marriage is lacking, we encourage you to look for opportunities to say to your spouse, "I am sorry I said _____ or did _____. I can see it was not helpful to you, and I would like to do things differently in the future. I am so sorry. Would you forgive me? Would you help me to do it better and let me know when I have failed or when I have gotten it right?" Can you see and feel the power in these few words to connect hearts? If you're willing to honor and respect your spouse and to communicate "You can trust me with your heart," it can be wonderfully healing to your marriage.

Never underestimate the power of forgiveness. The cross reminds us what ultimate love is: giving up self for another. The least we can do to strengthen our intimacy is to see our wrongs and to ask for forgiveness or be willing to let our spouse know they have hurt us and we are willing to forgive them. It's never too late, and contrary to what many believe, we *can* change! We pray that forgiveness will become a major part of your marriage and that as you begin to feel empathy for your partner, your heart will soften, your anger will melt into love and trust, and your intimacy will deepen.

SMALL BEGINNINGS

1. What does forgiveness look like in your marriage right now? Do you forgive? Do you need forgiveness?
2. Who have you forgiven in the last year? Was it a positive process?
3. When, if ever, have you felt empathy for your spouse or someone else? What did that feel like? Have you ever noticed someone feeling empathy for you?
4. If there are presently offenses in your marriage, can you identify them? What might be some first steps to practicing forgiveness in your marriage that you can take even if it means you take them on your own?

—— **12** ——

DIVING DEEP INTO AN INTIMATE MARRIAGE

Several years ago, Carrie and I were invited to speak at a marriage enrichment event in Maui, and after about two seconds of prayer we decided that God wanted us to accept the invitation. Actually we did spend more than two seconds thinking and praying about it, but once we saw that the calendar was clear we knew we were on our way.

It was on that trip that I got the bug to become a scuba diver. I took a half-day "Introduction to Diving" course offered by a dive shop in Lahaina. They taught us how to use the equipment, checked us out in the swimming pool, and then allowed us to dive offshore at no more than thirty feet deep. In those twenty-five minutes under water, I discovered a world of peace and calm and exquisite beauty that I had never experienced when I floated on the surface sucking air through a snorkel. I realized that floating on the surface was not nearly as exciting, amazing, and rewarding as actually diving into the water and experiencing fish, coral, and other aquatic life up close.

When I told Carrie of my newfound love, she was excited for me.

Note those last two words: *for me*. She was clear that if I wanted to learn how to dive I had her blessing, but there was NO WAY she was going to put all of that stuff on and go underwater where at any time a shark might appear. The thought of seeing a shark actually increased my desire to dive.

Well, with her blessing my good friend Chip and I took diving lessons. I enjoyed it so much that I went beyond my PADI Open Water Certification. I eventually earned a Master Scuba Diver and then the Divemaster certifications. Diving had become a place where I could relax, focus on the beauty around me, and in many ways be still and experience the majesty of my Lord. At first I kept on encouraging Carrie to learn how to dive so that she could be my dive buddy and we could dive together. But it quickly became clear that my invitations felt like pressure and weren't welcome, so I backed off.

Then one Father's Day I opened a card from Carrie, and in that card was one of the most precious gifts she's ever given to me. The card said that she knew how much I loved diving and how important it was for a diver to dive with a buddy. She wanted to be my "dive buddy" and, because of her love for me, was going to take diving lessons. Now, you need to understand that only a deep love could motivate my wife to learn how to dive in spite of her fear of sharks. Since that time we've been on a number of dives together, and some of our greatest memories of enjoying each other and experiencing God are from our diving trips.

Over the years we realized that there are some valuable lessons we learned in diving that we were able to apply to our marriage. Here are just a few of them:

GET GOOD TRAINING

IN DIVING

In order to be able to rent the equipment to dive you have to have a "C" card, which says you have obtained your Open Water Certification through one of the world's recognized diver training organizations. This training involves class time learning theory, understanding the equipment, becoming aware of the dangers and key safety procedures, and practicing core skills. You start by taking a class, listening to lectures, taking some tests, and watching videos. Then you get the equipment on and go into the shallow end of a swimming pool, so it's not life threatening if you make a mistake. At each step your instructor will make sure you are safe and know what you're doing. He or she will have you repeat the core skills several times. Then, once you get more comfortable, you move to the open water for more training and a final test.

IN MARRIAGE

Marriage is the most important and the most challenging relationship anyone can ever experience. It can also be the most fulfilling and the most rewarding. That's how God designed it to be. We don't have to have any special certification to be married, but God is the ultimate instructor. If we're willing to follow His lead, He will teach and guide us through His Word. He'll give us opportunities to learn and use relationship skills in marriage. And then He'll give us the opportunity to move into deeper levels of intimacy with each other, all the while making sure we are safe. There are a lot of valuable things God will show you to help you enjoy the kind of marriage you had in mind the day you said "I do."

DIVE WITH YOUR BUDDY

IN DIVING

One of the primary safety factors in diving is to dive with a buddy. The best buddy is someone you know, who is a certified diver, who takes diving seriously, who knows your strengths and weaknesses as a diver, and who watches out for you. Before you get in the water you help each other make sure your equipment is on right and working. When you are underwater, you never let your buddy out of sight. Never. You dive together, you enjoy the dive together, you remind each other to check the air supply, and if one of you gets in trouble, the other is always there, trained and ready to provide an alternate source of air and help you make a safe ascent to the surface. When you have a sense of safety that comes from having a dive buddy you can trust, it is much easier to relax and enjoy the dive.

IN MARRIAGE

While one person can make a difference in a marriage, it's always best to have two people who are committed to a deep, loving, Christ-centered, and intimate marriage. Amazing things can happen in a marriage when partners take their marriage seriously, know each other's strengths and weaknesses, and watch out for each other. Activities such as reading books together (such as *Mad About Us*), attending seminars and workshops, talking and praying together about your marriage, and sharing with other couples provide opportunities to increase your sense of personal safety, build trust and mutual satisfaction, and deepen your levels of intimacy.

PLAN YOUR DIVE AND DIVE YOUR PLAN

IN DIVING

Before you and your dive buddy get into the water it is absolutely essential that you plan your dive: where you are going to go, how deep you will go, how long you can stay at the deepest part of your dive, how much air you will need to have left in your tanks to make a safe ascent and allow for a reserve for safety, what the water conditions are, whether there is a current, whether it will be a drift dive—these are some of the important questions a wise diver asks before even thinking about putting on the mask, fins, diving vest, and air tanks. If you are diving in an area for the first time, it is wise to talk with someone who knows the area well so they can help you, or hire a Divemaster to lead the dive for you. The better you plan, the better you prepare, the better and safer and more enjoyable the dive, and the more likely you are to be able to dive again.

IN MARRIAGE

Most people plan for their education, their health, their home, and their finances, but very few people plan for their marriage. Most couples spend thousands of dollars preparing for their wedding and invest nothing in preparing for their marriage. Most people check the oil in their car more frequently than they check their marriage relationship. Do you have a plan for your marriage? What's important to you and your spouse? Has your marriage been growing or have you been in a holding pattern? Are you exercising your relationship skills or are they, like muscles that aren't exercised, experiencing some atrophy? Do you have regular times of prayer and conversation together? Do you have regular date nights without the kids? Do you read as many books on marriage as you do books on leadership or mystery or romance novels? When is the last time you attended a marriage enrichment conference and invested a weekend focusing on how to cultivate a deep and more intimate marriage relationship? What's your plan?

REVIEW YOUR DIVE

IN DIVING

After we've gotten out of the water and dried off, we've found it helpful to talk about the dive. What did we enjoy? What surprised us? What was uncomfortable? Was there anything either of us did or didn't do that made the other person feel unsafe or at risk? What would make the next dive even better? Sometimes we've come up with several helpful insights, and at other times we've just talked about what a great dive it was. By reviewing the dive and listening to what our partner has to say we are choosing to understand and value each other's perspective so that we can have an even better dive next time.

IN MARRIAGE

How much time do you spend talking about your marriage relationship? Do you ever discuss what you enjoy, what has surprised you, what is uncomfortable, what either of you do or don't do that makes the other person feel unsafe or at risk, and what you could do more of to let your beloved know that they are precious in your sight and first in your heart? When is the last time you complimented your spouse? When is the last time you thanked them for doing something they always do that makes your life a little easier? By looking at your marriage and listening to what your partner has to say, you are choosing to understand and value their perspective and increase their sense of safety and trust so that you can enjoy greater intimacy and passion in your marriage.

In your marriage relationship you can choose to be like the snorkeler who just floats on the surface and looks down at the magnificent, bright, and colorful underwater world below or you can take the hand of your "life buddy" and dive into all that God designed marriage to be and help you become. You can discover a new world of relational awe and wonder that many only read about. God's dive plan for marriage isn't a secret.

In Genesis we are told that God created man and woman to be in relationship with Him and with each other. Some people are amazed when they come to the part that says they were "naked and unashamed" (see Genesis 2:25). Why are some amazed? In the context of today's world it is amazing that two people could be so completely comfortable with each other that they are unashamed and vulnerable, not just sexually, but with their entire selves.

It's sad to read just a few verses later that after both had eaten of the forbidden fruit, they covered themselves to hide from each other and from God. The intimacy that had been so natural and automatic was suddenly replaced with hiding from God, themselves, and each other.

Hiding is what most of us know how to do. Sin caused us to go from naked and unashamed to naked and ashamed. The fact that people might see who we really are is what causes us to don our masks that help us hide, fake it, deny, conceal, and protect . . . even, and sometimes especially, in the marriage relationship.

Brennan Manning in his book *Abba's Child* calls this type of behavior putting on the imposter self. This imposter prevents us from communicating to another person who we really are and has little invested in seeing inside of someone else. Intimacy is an illusive concept to many of us. We are missing exactly what God designed us for: intimacy with Him first and then with each other—to know and be known, naked and unashamed.

God created us in His image. This means that, like Him, we can experience intimacy. On the human level that means the ability to be naked and unashamed with our mind, our will, and our emotions. A marriage has little chance of surviving if a couple doesn't grasp the importance of cultivating and growing intimacy. In fact, one of the most important tasks in the first few years of marriage is to understand what intimacy is and some of the practical things we can do to help intimacy thrive.

The key to having a great marriage isn't focusing on how to have a great marriage. It is focusing on what it means to love the Lord, serve the Lord, and allow God to help us become conformed to the image of His Son. What does it look like to love one another as Christ loved us? What does it look like to "bear all things, believe all things, hope all things, and endure all things" (1 Corinthians 13:7 NKJV)? What does it mean to be a servant? What does the Great Commandment look like in real life? The key to having a great marriage is focusing on specific things you can do to be a better spouse.

Albert Einstein once said: "Strange is our situation here on earth.

Each of us comes for a short visit, not knowing why, but sometimes seeming to a Divine purpose. There is one thing we do know definitively: that we are here for the sake of each other. Many times a day I realize how much my outer and inner life is built upon the labor of others, and how earnestly I must exert myself in order to give in return as much as I have received and am still receiving." It's true, we are here for the sake of each other.

Do you remember why you married your spouse? Do you remember when you proposed or when you said "I do"? What were your dreams, hopes, expectations? We were both Christians when we started dating. Gary had degrees from a Bible college and two seminaries, and Carrie had just graduated from the University of Nebraska. We loved the Lord, we loved each other, and we took our faith seriously. We went to church, tithed, were involved in Bible studies, and served in different church ministries. We wanted to spend our lives discovering and clarifying why we were created, why God gave us the education, opportunities, and experience that He did, why He brought us together, and how we could spend whatever years we had remaining on this earth serving the Lord. We looked forward to growing old together.

Although having children and being good parents was one of our biggest shared values, we believed that God had brought us together for a purpose beyond procreating. While we wanted to be financially secure, own a home, and not be in debt, we knew God had brought us together for more than just being safe. We knew Christ didn't die and rise again and then bring us together as a couple just to be comfortable.

We've moved four times in our marriage, and all of our moves have been made with the sense that God was leading us to a place where somehow we could be more effective for the kingdom of God. Some of our moves didn't make sense financially, emotionally, or relationally. Our last move was one we didn't want to make but knew that God wanted us to make. Several of our moves took us farther away from extended family, and being close to at least one of our families was something we both placed a very high value on. But for some reason that wasn't what happened. But what has happened is that as we've tried to be faithful to God's leading in our lives and cultivate a Christ-centered marriage, God has given us the wisdom to listen through the anger to the deeper emotions in each other's hearts, and we've mustered the courage to learn how to manage conflicts in healthy ways. As a result we have, by God's grace, experienced a growing love, passion, and depth of intimacy that was beyond our comprehension when we stood at the altar and said "I do."

Our twenty-six years of marriage have been quite an adventure of faith. The book you've just read includes some of the "greatest hits" of what God has taught us. Some of the lessons we've learned quickly, and some have come with a great deal of pain, but ALL of the lessons have deepened our capacity to experience great joy, increasing love, and deep levels of intimacy. Change and growth always begin with the first step. Regardless of what your spouse chooses to do, what one thing are you willing to do to help you develop a "Mad About Us" marriage?

SMALL BEGINNINGS

1. Is there an activity your spouse enjoys that you don't appreciate as much? Find out what your spouse enjoys about it.

2. What kind of preparation did you have for your marriage? What was the most helpful about it?

3. What do you know now about marriage that you didn't know before you got married?

4. Plan to do at least one thing as a couple to improve your marriage, such as study this book together or go to a marriage conference together.

5. Regardless of what your partner does, what will you do differently in the next three to six months to become a better spouse?

EPILOGUE

I would like to tell you the story of my journey from anger, through conflict, to intimacy. Who am I? A name or gender doesn't matter, for I represent every person who has ever married. This is my story, but it can be yours as well. I am sharing with you not only my thoughts but also from my heart and many years of real-life experience. It's a story of the surprising pathway to intimacy, everyone's dream for their marriage. I now realize that as an image bearer of God himself, I can experience and enjoy all that God designed marriage to be. An intimate and mutually satisfying marriage is not some unachievable fantasy—it can become a reality. It did for me.

I used to believe that all conflict was wrong and that anger was always a bad emotion and a barrier to my intimacy with God as well as my spouse. But then I discovered it can be just the opposite. Strange as it seems, it can actually be a pathway to deep levels of intimacy if we let it. But during the first years of our marriage unhealthy anger and fear of conflict distanced us from each other rather than drew us closer. That wasn't anger's fault, it was ours. It was due to a misuse and lack of understanding of the emotion.

As I look back I guess we entered marriage naïve and a bit blind. We thought we knew each other—I mean, really knew each other— but in so many ways, we each married a stranger. We each wanted a soul mate with instant intimacy. But so many times we asked ourselves, *Who is this person? I don't know him/her—I thought I did, but this person feels strange and very unsafe.*

Our intimacy came and then vanished just as quickly. That fed our hurts, fears, and frustrations and increased our tendency to avoid or attack. I guess we both expected the other to just magically know what we needed and fulfill it automatically, but that didn't happen. Neither of us was a mind reader. That too fed those primary emotions, which fed the anger and triggered the conflicts.

Because of my background I needed my spouse to be everything my parents weren't. It was difficult to trust, so I needed someone totally trustworthy. I wanted a partner who would be totally honest. I wanted someone who would always (and I mean always) be accepting and forgiving of my slip-ups, who would always assume the best and know that deep down inside I was really a kind, thoughtful, and wonderful person. That also meant she wouldn't be angry or upset with me. And finally, I needed a spouse who understood the meaning of boundaries and would respect mine.

Well, by now you've got the picture. "Superspouse" didn't exist except in my own mind. When my spouse didn't meet my unrealistic expectations, it fueled more hurt and frustration and fear. And my unhealthy—and at times selfish and immature—reactions fed his as well. The funny thing is, and it's somewhat embarrassing to admit this, I never once thought about the fact that maybe my spouse was looking for me to be a superspouse too—I only thought about how my spouse didn't meet my needs. I never (that's right, never) thought about how I wasn't meeting his.

Since then I've learned that these traits develop and grow *during* marriage. People don't come prepackaged with them. They aren't instantly in place. Becoming a true soul mate doesn't happen overnight.

During the first ten to fifteen years of marriage we didn't really build much intimacy; we built barriers. My mind grabbed, held on to, and expanded each offense. I hate to admit this, but over time I expected the person I loved—the person I married and committed to spending the rest of my life with—NOT to come through in the way I wanted and thought I needed. Well, by now you know what happened. That just fed more of my hurt, frustration, and fear and led to more conflicts, which made us both feel more unsafe, decreased our trust, and eroded what little intimacy we did have. What a dysfunctional and vicious cycle. And what does this say about me!

Okay, now here is some encouraging news. I've discovered a few simple truths. I've learned some things about God, about myself, and about anger and conflict and intimacy. It's really rather simple. Real change and growth in marriage starts with me. *It starts with me.*

I've learned how to apply Psalm 139:23–24: "Search me, O God, and know my heart; test me and know my anxious thoughts. See if there is any offensive way in me, and lead me in the way everlasting." The only person I can control is me. The only person I can change is me. Real intimacy starts with my choices: choosing to be understanding, choosing to be trustworthy, choosing to be honest, choosing to be forgiving and respectful of boundaries. Intimacy doesn't come prepackaged. Intimacy isn't a result of a marital microwave but is the result of a marriage marinated slowly in love, patience, understanding, and massive doses of prayer.

Yes, prayer. I knew that prayer was important, that the Bible had a lot to say about prayer, that we "have not because we ask not" (see James 4:2), that God promised to answer the prayers of His people, etc. But apart from meals and other spiritually appropriate times, I didn't pray. And WE didn't pray. Too awkward. Too uncomfortable. Too foreign. Too unnecessary. Besides that, I knew a number of other married Christians, and they didn't pray with their spouses, so on a practical level it really couldn't be THAT important. But it is. I was wrong. And now I understand that prayer changes the people who pray and what they pray about. It doesn't matter whether I feel like it or not, it is a vital part of my relationship with God and with my spouse. God has used prayer to transform me and my marriage.

I used to resist and resent my spouse's differences. That created barriers, diminished intimacy, and fed my anger. One day I woke up and realized, "I didn't marry a clone, and I don't want to be married to a replica of me." It was when I began to celebrate our differences and thanked God for my spouse's uniqueness that we drew closer. After I began to change, my spouse began to respond, and we learned some phrases that changed our interaction. Perhaps these could help you in your journey:

"I want to see this situation or problem through your eyes. Will you help me do that?"

"I'm sorry that I didn't really listen to what you said earlier. I was afraid it would lead to conflict. While it may be uncomfortable for me, I really do want to understand you. Would you give me another chance?"

"When we have a disagreement, what could I do that would make it easier for you to feel free to be really open with me?"

"Thank you for sharing your anger with me. While it's a bit threatening to me, I know there is a message there and I want to understand it so that I can understand you."

Now, that last one was the hardest to say. But what a difference it made in our relationship! I discovered that to be really intimate I have to try to see things through my spouse's eyes and feel things with my spouse's heart and she, hopefully, will do the same.

I also learned to ask, "What do I do when I'm angry that makes it difficult for you to feel close to me?" A breakthrough came for us when we asked each other to take the time to respond to these questions in writing. What a revelation! Sometimes what is very hard to hear and not react to is much easier to "hear" when you are reading it. We could have gone on for years and never discovered what we found by doing this.

A big discovery was about our emotions. They're good. They're a gift. God gave them to us to enrich our lives and relationships. Denying or ignoring them doesn't work. They find a way out. Always. No exceptions. Whenever I bury an emotion it is buried alive, and it will come out sooner or later in some way, shape, or form.

So we began to learn a feeling vocabulary. We made a game out of this. We decided to see how many different feeling words we could name, and then we had to come up with a word picture for each one. For example, one of my word pictures for feeling depressed is what I felt when I was young and I was told that my grandpa had just died. One of my spouse's most powerful word pictures for fear was when as a little child being stuck in an elevator all alone for almost half an hour and not knowing if they would ever get out. If it's true that "feelings are the currency of intimacy," I want to be aware of my emotions and share them in ways that will lead to better understanding.

For many years I wondered why I had so much anger toward the one I loved the most. Then I discovered that my question contained the answer—it's because of that depth of love that I have deeper emotions. Love and anger aren't opposites. They're intertwined and can trigger one another, and they have. It took me time to see this as well as come out straight with my anger. My family used every form of anger expression imaginable, so I grew up confused about anger as well as wanting to avoid it. This didn't work. Stuffing or repressing it is emotional suicide. I tried to get rid of it. Not a chance. Now that I understand it, it's like a friend who needs to be handled carefully.

It was so freeing for me to learn to be a mature responder. I overcame my fear of anger when I learned that it was a God-given emotion that had potential for good; it was a secondary emotion, and I could choose to *respond* to the primary emotion and not *react* to the anger.

I had to learn to really listen not only to my spouse but to myself as well. I didn't always like how I sounded. Now I ask myself, "Do I sound angry or lovingly truthful?" There's a big difference.

After all these years our anger is working for us in a positive way. That may sound unbelievable to you, but it's true. Anger can be healthy rather than unhealthy. No longer do I say, "You make me angry." Rather, "I am angry because . . ." and I'm heard. In doing this I become a safe person for both of us. And this safety has increased our trust and has brought us closer together. Intimacy is no longer an infrequent visitor or guest, but more of a permanent resident in our marriage.

We now have a new approach as we look at our marriage. It used to be "What's broken and how can we fix it?" Now it's "What's working and how can we make it work better?" We used to be problem-focused, but over time we've learned how to be growth-focused. And that in itself reduces unhealthy anger that so often would have sabotaged any hope of constructive conflict.

Conflict. That word used to scare the dickens out of me. I avoided it like the plague. So did everyone in the family I came from. While conflict is still not one of my favorite things, I've learned that there is such a thing as healthy conflict. I've learned that it's not about winning or losing but seizing the opportunity for understanding and insight that can increase safety and produce the levels of trust that allow real intimacy to flourish.

I know we will not always agree. That's all right. Disagreement is no longer a threat to our marriage or our intimacy. It's now constructive. We ask each other, "How can we make this disagreement work for us instead of against us? What do you think and feel? I want to listen to you so that I can understand you." My need to control has diminished and so has theirs. "Power struggles are us" used to be our motto. But that has changed, and now we try to discover how we can better serve each other. Now we feel as though both of us win rather than both lose. Conflict is no longer a negative that sends us two steps back in our marriage; now it moves us forward. We do a review after every conflict and ask, "What did we learn from this and how will we be different?" We still have a ways to go with how we handle conflict, but we have turned a significant corner and spend much more time being mad *about* each other than mad *at* each other.

My prayers for my spouse have changed radically. They're no longer self-centered. ("Lord, help my spouse to change.") Now they're other-centered. ("Help me to understand where my spouse is coming from" and "Help me to set aside my opinion in order to better understand my spouse's.") This can be a powerful prelude to intimacy.

I also pray that God will help me communicate my anger in ways that honor my spouse, glorify Him, and actually become an expression of my love for my beloved. Well, that's my journey so far. I've come a ways and I still have further to go. It's been worthwhile, but not without pain and discomfort. Perhaps you have some lingering questions about me. Do I always get it right? No way. Do I always embrace conflict and disagreements? Of course not. Do I always like anger? No. But it's here. It's an inevitable part of every marriage relationship, so why fight it? Why not learn how to make it work for you rather than against you? If I can learn to understand it, accept it, use it, grow from its existence, and become more intimate, so can you.

When we got married we were madly in love. We were mad about each other. We couldn't get enough of each other. Then for a long time we were just mad. I mean really mad. Mad at ourselves, mad at each other, and mad at God. Now, by God's grace and a lot of hard work, we are once again madly in love and enjoying an intimacy we never dreamed possible. Really! Through God's presence in our lives, the power of prayer, and the willingness to take personal responsibility to be the best spouse possible, our marriage is better and stronger than we ever dreamed possible. Are you willing to take the time to make the choices and take personal responsibility for making this happen in your marriage? Are you willing, regardless of what your spouse chooses to do, to take the first steps?

GET READY TO LEAD

If you're reading this leader's preparation section, you're getting ready to stare into multiple sets of eyeballs that are expecting something significant! It's small group time—and a couples' group can raise the stakes even more. A few simple principles will launch you into success as a small group leader.

WHO'S LEARNING WHAT?

A small group functions on multiple levels. Individuals come with hearts and minds open to varying degrees. Some will take away a great deal from the group, some will take less. Along the way you may see some individuals open up and become engaged with more energy than they begin with. That's a pleasant by-product of the time you spend together.

Not only does individual learning happen, but the group bonds. Some people will participate because they're looking for friends, even if subconsciously. Surface relationships go to a new level. Group members become friends as they learn about each other's lives and spend time praying for each other. Many people in churches attribute some of their deepest friendships to having experienced a small group together.

Because this is a couples' group that focuses on issues that surface in marriage, it's also an opportunity for change to happen in those marriages. You may not see changes immediately because the inner workings of a marriage are so private. But as facilitator of a couples' discussion group, you have the privilege of setting the stage and creating a climate where it is safe for group members to explore change at deep levels.

WHO'S THERE?

Good news! At least one person in each couple wants to be in your group! Voluntary participation is a key first step in adult learning and in bringing about life change. Small groups are not court-ordered, so you've already got a great stepping stone to discussion that will make an impact.

Many adult learners have been conditioned to expect to learn by listening to someone talk. This is not the most effective learning method for any age, but as students get older, most of them learn how to behave in this kind of setting. In large groups, we even take it for granted that we will listen to someone else talk. But this is a small group—so it's a wonderful opportunity to experience more participatory learning. As you plan each session, remember to take advantage of this dynamic.

Adults are motivated to learn when there's something in it for them. Some people truly do love learning for the sake of learning, but most busy adults want clear take-away value for the time and effort they invest. They want to be able to apply what they've learned, to see something change as a result of what they've learned.

Adult learners also tend to appreciate groups or settings where they are confident they have a contribution to make. A small group is a key opportunity to welcome input from a variety of people and thereby make the group more interesting for everyone.

Key to a comfortable discussion setting is the ability of the facilitator to put everyone on equal footing. Aim to remove unspoken requirements of prior knowledge or experience. Ask questions in ways that flatten the playing field and allow everyone to respond without fearing that they're giving a wrong or inferior answer.

WHO'S IN CHARGE HERE?

While a small group discussion format means that the facilitator doesn't have to have all the answers all the time, the leader can be prepared for some of the dynamics that impact everyone's experience of the group.

Group size: A group of about four to six couples is likely to be conducive to discussion and relationship building. This is a good size for everyone to feel like part of the group. A larger group allows for the possibility of people feeling on the fringe—or even intentionally staying on the fringe. A smaller group may make people feel like they're "on the spot."

Time: Respect people's time. Start when you say you plan to start, and finish when you promised to finish. As the group grows and changes together, you can discern what level of flexibility is acceptable, but in the beginning be sure to deliver what you promised.

Personalities: Obviously you'll have a mix of personality types. Make a point to make everyone feel welcome, not showing preference to those who are quick to answer your questions or with whom you already have a connection. Look for opportunities to gently direct group members toward each other, keeping your eyes and ears open to what they may have in common with each other and not be aware of.

Stay on topic: Every small group has the potential to go off the topic—or never get around to the topic at all. It's the facilitator's job to make sure the group does what you agreed you would do together. Sometimes this means simply saying, "Thank you, Steve. Let's look at question three now." If Steve's comment was off topic, resist the temptation to follow him down that trail.

Participation: A verbal extrovert is obviously more likely to jump in and answer a question than an introvert who likes to think things through a little bit. Don't put people on the spot to participate in uncomfortable ways, but do look for opportunities to include the quiet types. Often you'll notice something in their facial expression or a change of position that alerts you that an individual is mentally engaged and may be working up to saying something out loud. It might be that all it takes is, "Do you have any thoughts, Karen?" You can also involve quiet group members in nonthreatening ways such as asking them to read a chapter summary or Scripture passage aloud.

Be prepared: As a facilitator, don't fall into the trap of thinking you can lead a discussion on the fly. Do the same thing you hope participants will do—read the chapter in advance and consider personal answers to the discussion questions that appear at the end of each chapter. But also seek ways to apply what you've read in your own life. Then prayerfully prepare your heart for each session. Pray that God might give you wisdom and discernment as you facilitate not just a discussion but a genuine growth opportunity for all of the participants. You might even enlist two or three friends to covenant to pray for you at least once a day that God might help you have a prepared mind and a prepared heart. Remember, the purpose of the discussion isn't just to get the right answer but to encourage and motivate each participant to find practical ways to apply at least one thing to their marriage in the coming week.

In each individual session, and over the course of eleven sessions together talking about *Mad About Us,* group members will move from fuzzy befuddlement to "aha!" moments as new principles sink in. Celebrate your growth together and give thanks to God for each member of your group.

SESSION 1:
And they lived happily ever after

Invite brief general responses to chapter 1. What's one thing they might have already applied in their own marriage this week? Then ask a volunteer to read the chapter summary aloud.

God's design for marriage is that we experience intimacy with Him and then with each other. He wants us to be transformed in the marriage relationship, so that each day we would look just a little bit more like Him because we spent the day with our spouse. When we are functioning out of what God planned for us we experience deeper and deeper levels of intimacy both with Him and each other.

Discuss these questions:

1. Identify the disappointments of the "ever after" that many couples experience.
2. What are some differences that seem to plague marriage relationships? What about differences that spouses enjoy?
3. How would you describe intimacy? What about intimacy in marriage?
4. How can a married couple allow Jesus to come into their relationship more fully?
   Read and discuss Genesis 2:18–24.
5. How does this passage contribute to your understanding of intimacy in marriage?
6. Share your ideas about God's design for intimacy in marriage.

Close with prayer. Offer a time for your group to pray for one another, then close with a prayer like this one:

Lord, you had something beautiful in mind when you brought man and woman together. Remind us to look to you for our understanding of marriage, not to the world's ideas. Draw us closer to you, so that as we experience intimacy with you, we will also experience intimacy with each other. Amen.

SESSION 2:
Designed to experience intimacy

Invite brief, general responses to chapter 2. What's one thing they might have already applied in their own marriage this week? Then ask a volunteer to read the chapter summary aloud.

We were built with a need for connection, to bond, to belong.

Intimacy is something that has to be cultivated, attended to, watered, and cared for. Intimacy begins with understanding that we are designed in God's image, and that we can trust Him with all of our daily experiences. Honesty, forgiveness, and godly boundaries are all important components to building an intimate relationship with a spouse.

Discuss these questions:

1. What is your definition of intimacy?
2. Which component of intimacy mentioned in this chapter do you think is difficult for many people (sense of self, trust, honesty, forgiveness, boundaries)? Why?
3. What holds married people back from risking intimacy?
4. What might be some possible ways to improve intimacy in marriage in a few weeks' time?
   Read and discuss Proverbs 3:5 and Psalm 22:8.
5. How can trusting God help build intimacy in marriage?
6. How has the Lord "rescued" or "delivered" you in your marriage?

Close with prayer. Offer a time for your group to pray for one another, then close with a prayer like this one:

Lord, you are the one we trust. Help us in our moments of doubt to turn to you for true hope. Help us be honest and forgiving in our marriage relationships. Make us into the trustworthy people you want us to be. Amen.

SESSION 3:
Barriers to intimacy

Invite brief, general responses to chapter 3. What's one thing they might have already applied in their own marriage this week? Then ask a volunteer to read the chapter summary aloud.

In the initial years of marriage how we interpret each other is important to our not building barriers to the very intimacy we want. Usually lurking right behind a barrier is anger stemming from some type of hurt, fear, or frustration. As long as the barrier is in place, we will not move through it to intimacy. Intimacy requires that we know each other more deeply with time. Intimacy can improve right away in a marriage and barriers can begin to come down if even one person makes a decision to do something differently.

Discuss these questions:

1. What are some barriers to intimacy in marriage?
2. Do you think men and women face different barriers to intimacy? Explain.
3. What is the difference between a reactive spirit and a responsive spirit?
4. What gets in the way of deciding that you want things to change?

   The authors remind us of Joshua 1:9. Read this verse aloud, then discuss this question.
5. How would you apply this verse to barriers to intimacy in marriage?

Close with prayer. Offer a time for your group to pray for one another, then close with a prayer like this one:

Lord, we are fearful people, and we let our fear get in the way of what you want for us. Give us the courage to be willing to change, to take the first step toward taking down the barriers that prevent us from having the closeness you designed for marriage. In Jesus' name, amen.

SESSION 4:
The emotional side of intimacy

Invite brief, general responses to chapter 4. What's one thing they might have already applied in their own marriage this week? Then ask a volunteer to read the chapter summary aloud.

It doesn't take newlyweds long to discover that the precious intimacy they thought would come easily can be quickly broken. Many Christians have emphasized the mind and the will to the exclusion of emotions. But we have emotions because God has emotions and we are made in His image. Our emotions influence almost every aspect of our lives. Sin has led to unhealthy ways to deal with our emotions, but by God's grace we can find healthy responses.

Discuss these questions:

1. What did you learn about emotions from the way you were raised? Were there differences between how boys and girls were expected to express emotions? What were some of those differences?

2. Review the list of common emotions in the chapter. Which ones do you identify with the most?

3. How do emotions control us if we don't understand and control them?

4. How can attitudes about emotions affect the marriage relationship both positively and negatively?

   Read and discuss Romans 8:28–29.

5. In what ways does the marriage experience help us be conformed to the image of Jesus?

Close with prayer. Offer a time for your group to pray for one another, then close with a prayer like this one:

Lord, we carry our past with us whether we realize it or not. So sometimes emotional patterns we've learned when we were younger affect the way we related to people we love. Remind us that nothing is beyond your redeeming power. Redeem our emotions, and make them an arena where we see your power displayed. Amen.

SESSION 5:
From intimacy to anger

Invite brief, general responses to chapter 5. What's one thing they might have already applied in their own marriage this week? Then ask a volunteer to read the chapter summary aloud.

Many people really believe that healthy couples don't have conflict. But research tells us that happily married couples disagree almost as much as unhappily married couples. This difference is that their disagreements result in increased understanding, trust, and intimacy. Anger is a God-given emotion, and it is not always negative. Healthy anger has tremendous potential for good.

Discuss these questions:

1. Before reading this chapter, did you think anger was a negative or a positive emotion? Explain.
2. Describe what experiences in your life might have set you up or made you more vulnerable to experiencing the emotion of anger.
3. What might be three potentially positive aspects of healthy anger for the marriage relationship?
4. Identify at least one thing you learned in this chapter that will help change how you manage your anger.
   Read and discuss Proverbs 16:32 and James 1:19–20.
5. What do these verses teach us about our anger?
6. What impact does anger have on our relationship with God?

Close with prayer. Offer a time for your group to pray for one another, then close with a prayer like this one:

Lord, you understand our emotions better than we do. Teach us what we can learn from our own anger and how to use it to build intimacy in our marriages. Amen.

SESSION 6:
The myths of anger

Invite brief, general responses to chapter 6. What's one thing they might have already applied in their own marriage this week? Then ask a volunteer to read the chapter summary aloud.

Anger is a complex emotion. It can disguise itself in many ways, and our society has sanctioned misunderstandings about anger that keep us from using anger in healthy ways. Anger myths build walls of fear, indifference, distance, and shame. Even one myth can have a negative impact on building understanding and intimacy in marriage.

Discuss these questions:

1. Review the list of anger myths in the chapter. Which one stands out the most to you personally? Why?
2. Which of these myths do you think is most prevalent in our society at large? Explain.
3. What happens in marriage relationships when we believe any of these myths?
4. What steps can married people take to break down the impact of these myths in their relationship?
   Read and discuss Ephesians 4:26–27.
5. What important truths do these verses teach us?

Close with prayer. Offer a time for your group to pray for one another, then close with a prayer like this one:

Lord, we experience emotions because you created us in your image. Emotions, including anger, are complex, and in our humanness, they get the best of us sometimes. Show us the truth about anger. Show us the damage that believing lies has done to our marriages. Show us what you want us to understand about anger, so that we can be more like you. Amen.

SESSION 7:
The many faces of anger

Invite brief, general responses to chapter 7. What's one thing they might have already applied in their own marriage this week? Then ask a volunteer to read the chapter summary aloud.

Anger is a God-given emotion that can be experienced and expressed in healthy and unhealthy ways. Sometimes our emotional patterns are so automatic they are hard to identify. The first step is to identify our characteristic styles of experiencing and expressing anger. Then we can move from reacting in unhealthy ways to responding in healthy ways. The mature response to anger can transform our marriage relationships.

Discuss these questions:

1. Review the cream puff, locomotive, and steel magnolia patterns of reacting to anger. Which of these patterns did you see around you as you grew up?
2. What effect do you think the patterns of your parents had on you as you developed your own patterns?
3. What do you think is the difference between reacting and responding? How do you feel when someone reacts to you? How do you feel when someone responds to you?
4. What's one thing you could do this week that would be a healthy change in your own anger patterns?
   Read and discuss Hebrews 12:15.
5. What does this verse tell us can happen if we don't recognize our anger patterns?
6. What must happen for us to allow God to deal with the root causes of our anger?

Close with prayer. Offer a time for your group to pray for one another, then close with a prayer like this one:

Lord God, we don't always like the truth when we finally see it. Give us the courage to look at our anger patterns and honestly acknowledge the effects negative anger patterns have on our relationships. We look to you, the source of transformation, to help us change reactions to responses that honor you. In Jesus' name, amen.

SESSION 8:
Making anger work for you

Invite brief, general responses to chapter 8. What's one thing they might have already applied in their own marriage this week? Then ask a volunteer to read the chapter summary aloud.

Change is possible! With God's help, we can learn to make our God-given emotion of anger work for us rather than against us. We can learn how to invest our anger energy in constructive responses rather than spend it in destructive reactions. This doesn't happen overnight, but the starting point in the change process is to recognize our need to change and ask God to help us take responsibility to make the first step.

Discuss these questions:

1. What keeps us from taking responsibility for our own anger patterns?
2. In what ways is anger an automatic defense mechanism for many people?
3. What are some common emotions or attitudes underlying anger?
4. Can you think of a time when your anger was a false alarm? What can you learn from that situation?
   Read and discuss Psalm 139:23–24.
5. How do these verses show that David was taking personal responsibility for his own patterns? What did he do and say?
6. In your own words, say what you'd like God to search your heart for.

Close with prayer. Offer a time for your group to pray for one another, then close with a prayer like this one:

Heavenly Father, it's so much easier to blame someone else! Search our hearts and reveal to us the lessons we need to learn so that we can make our anger work for us instead of against us in our marriage relationships. We pray in Jesus' name, amen.

SESSION 9:
Intimate conflict: a pathway to intimacy

Invite brief, general responses to chapter 9. What's one thing they might have already applied in their own marriage this week? Then ask a volunteer to read the chapter summary aloud.

It can take married people many years to learn the value of healthy conflict. Our differences—when understood, appreciated, and allowed to be used by God—can actually enrich our lives and marriage relationships. This process of rubbing lives together day after day, month after month, year after year, becomes God's change agent. This refining tool helps us to understand our own emotions and when we can and can't trust them, gives us understanding, teaches us acceptance, and helps us to change.

Discuss these questions:

1. Review the conflict styles described in the chapter. What kind of conflict styles did you see growing up?
2. What keeps married couples from pursuing healthy conflict styles with each other? What excuses do they use?
3. What is the cost of not dealing with conflict in marriage?
4. What are the benefits of constructively dealing with conflict in marriage?
   Read and discuss Romans 15:5–7.
5. How can you apply these verses to how you do conflict that might help it be more constructive?
6. How can these verses help one spouse respond to the other spouse's style?

Close with prayer. Offer a time for your group to pray for one another, then close with a prayer like this one:

Lord Jesus, you are our example. It's easy for us to learn destructive styles of dealing with conflict from the people around us, but what we want is to learn humble, healing style that you teach us. Amen.

SESSION 10:
Seven simple steps through conflict to intimacy

Invite brief, general responses to chapter 10. What's one thing they might have already applied in their own marriage this week? Then ask a volunteer to read the chapter summary aloud.

The best time to start dealing with conflict is before a conflict arises. Conflict is something that most people avoid, yet it is inevitable. Constructive conflict management is always easier when you have a plan. This starts with acknowledging there is a problem and determining how important it is. And as much as we hate to admit it, both partners contribute to conflict. We've run from it, hid from it, fought about it, cried over it—now it's time to resolve the issues that keep intimacy from growing in our marriages.

Discuss these questions:

1. How do you decide if an issue is high ticket or low ticket? What was one of your low-ticket items you experienced this week?
2. What sometimes keeps us from admitting our own contributions to conflict?
3. What factors might make it difficult for us to ask for forgiveness from our spouses?
4. What factors might cause us to hesitate to choose to change ourselves?

The authors remind us of the importance of seeking understanding. Read and discuss Proverbs 2:2–3; 3:13; 4:1; 4:7; and 19:8.

5. What kind of active participation do these verses identify in the process of seeking understanding?

6. What do these verses teach us about listening to our spouses? What will you do this week to become a doer and not only a hearer of what these verses teach?

Close with prayer. Offer a time for your group to pray for one another, then close with a prayer like this one:

Lord, we have so much noise in our lives that sometimes we have trouble listening to the people who matter most to us. Remind us to carve out time and space to set aside distractions and our own desires in order to listen to the people we love. In your name we pray, amen.

SESSION 11:
Forgiveness: the healing oil of intimacy

Invite brief, general responses to chapter 11. What's one thing they might have already applied in their own marriage this week? Then ask a volunteer to read the chapter summary aloud.

Forgiveness is essential in order for any relationship to keep growing and for trust to deepen. Forgiveness is the avenue, the path we must walk down if we are to let go of anger, resentment, and negativity toward our spouses, which almost always hinders intimacy. Forgiveness propels us forward. Lack of forgiveness keeps us wounded and stuck in the past.

Discuss these questions:

1. What makes forgiveness hard in some situations? Why do you think some find it almost impossible to take responsibility for what they've done, make a sincere apology, and ask for forgiveness?

2. Describe some wounds that married people may have a hard time letting go of. What are some of the short-term and long-term consequences of not letting go?
3. Tell about a time you had a positive experience of forgiving someone.
4. Do *forgive* and *forget* mean the same thing? Explain.
   Read and discuss Colossians 3:12–14.
5. How can applying this verse keep us from accumulating wounds?
6. How does our experience of the Lord's forgiveness impact the marriage relationship?

Close with prayer. Offer a time for your group to pray for one another, then close with a prayer like this one:

Lord, in our human weakness, forgiveness is a hard thing to do. We harbor hurts; sometimes we even make our own wounds bleed again. Give us an encounter with forgiveness that will transform us. Make us truly understand the depth of your forgiveness of us, so that we can forgive each other. Amen.

SESSION 12:
Diving deep into an intimate marriage

Invite brief general responses to Chapter 12. Then ask a volunteer to read the chapter summary aloud.

Most couples spend thousands of dollars preparing for their wedding and invest nothing in preparing for their marriage. Most people check the oil in their car more frequently than they check their marriage relationship. The key to having a great marriage isn't focusing on how to have a great marriage. It is focusing on what it means to love the Lord, serve the Lord, and allow God to help us become conformed to the image of His Son. What does it look like to love one another as Christ loved us?

Discuss these questions:

1. If you were telling an engaged couple how to train for marriage, what would you say?
2. Describe a favorite "buddy dive" you've had in your marriage.
3. What steps can a newly married couple take to plan their marriage? How about a couple married a long time?
4. Make a list of possible ways you could review your marriage.

Read and discuss 1 Corinthians 13:7.

5. Which of the characteristics described in this verse is the hardest for you to believe is true? Why?
6. What's the most encouraging thing this verse says about love?

Close with prayer. Offer a time for your group to pray for one another, then close with a prayer like this one:

Lord, you are the buddy who is with us on even the most scary dives of marriage. You are the Divemaster. Help us to remember to turn to you when we need reminders for how to have good dives in our marriage relationships. Keep us humble and teachable, no matter how long we've been married. Amen.

ENDNOTES

Chapter 1

1. Michael Gurian, *What Could He Be Thinking?* (New York: St. Martin's Press, 2003), chapter 3.
2. Ibid., 84.

Chapter 3

1. Patricia Love and Steven Stosny, *How to Improve Your Marriage Without Talking About It* (New York: Broadway, 2007), 141.

Chapter 4

1. Dorothy C. Finkelhor, *How to Make Your Emotions Work for You* (Berkeley: Medallion Books, 1973), 23–24.
2. John Powell, *Why Am I Afraid to Tell You Who I Am?* (Chicago: Argus, 1969), 25.

Chapter 5

1. Robert McCloskey, *Make Way for Ducklings* (New York: Viking Press, 1969).
2. *www.childhelp.org/resources/learning-center/statistics.* Accessed 8/1/07.
3. *www.ojp.usdoj.gov/bjs/homicide/relationship.htm.* Accessed 8/1/07.
4. *www.ojp.usdoj.gov/bjs/homicide/leok.htm.* Accessed 8/1/07.
5. *www.endabuse.org/resources/facts/.* Accessed 8/1/07.
6. G. E. Vaillant, *Adaptation to Life* (Boston: Little, Brown, 1977).
7. Harriet Lerner, *The Dance of Anger* (New York: Harper & Row, 1985), 1.
8. Matthew McKay, Peter Rogers, and Judith McCay, *When Anger Hurts* (Oakland, CA: New Harbinger, 2003), 25–26.

Chapter 6

1. Susan Peck, "Mission of Madness," *Long Beach Telegram*, December 18, 1987.
2. The anger myths are adapted from *A Woman's Forbidden Emotion* by H. Norman Wright and Gary J. Oliver, PhD (Ventura, CA: Regal Books, 2005), 61–72. Used by permission.
3. Here's what we came up with for Anger Fact #3: Anger is a God-given

emotion that can be expressed in healthy or unhealthy ways. Unhealthy expressions of anger are destructive and can lead to violence, while healthy expressions can actually be constructive and lead to increased understanding, trust, and intimacy.

4. Williams and Williams, *Anger Kills* (New York: Random House, 1993); Howard Kassinove, ed., *Anger Disorders* (Philadelphia: Taylor & Francis, 1995).
5. Joseph Cooke, *Free for the Taking* (Old Tappan, NJ: Fleming H. Revell Company, 1975), 109–10.
6. "Violent World of Woody Hayes," *Time* magazine, January 15, 1979.
7. Carol Tavris, *Anger: The Misunderstood Emotion* (New York: Touchstone Books, 1982).

Chapter 7

1. The anger styles are adapted from *A Woman's Forbidden Emotion* by Wright and Oliver. Used by permission.
2. John Lee, MAN! Men's Issues, Relationships, and Recovery Newsletter, No. 9 (Dec. 1990): 13.
3. Susan Jacoby, "Why Is That Lady So Red in the Face?" *McCall's*, Vol. 112 (Nov. 1983): 123ff.
4. Sonya Friedman, *Smart Cookies Don't Crumble* (New York: G. P. Putnam's Sons, 1985), 89–90.
5. Richard P. Walters, *Anger: Yours and Mine, and What to Do About It* (Zondervan: Grand Rapids, 1981), 17, 139.

Chapter 8

1. The anger curve is adapted from *A Woman's Forbidden Emotion* by Wright and Oliver. Used by permission.
2. Lerner, p. 13.
3. H. Norman Wright, *Always Daddy's Girl* (Ventura, CA: Regal Books, 1989), 218.
4. David Augsburger, *Be All You Can Be* (Carol Stream, IL: Creation House, 1970).

Chapter 11

1. Everett Worthington, *Handbook of Forgiveness* (Downers Grove, IL: InterVarsity Press, revised edition, 2003), 41.

ACKNOWLEDGMENTS

Thanks to our children, Nathan, Matt, and Andrew, who over the years helped us see the consequences of unhealthy anger and the value of healthy conflict in our marriage and family. You helped us know when we were getting it wrong and encouraged us when we got it right.

Thanks to our special team at The Center for Relationship Enrichment at John Brown University for thinking out loud with us and responding to various portions of the manuscript, and a special thanks to Jan Phillips and Greg Smalley for their contributions.

Thanks to Jane, Lonnie, Wendy, and their husbands, and to other dear friends for their faithful encouragement, prayers, and support, to Ehab and Sylvie and our other Houston friends who gave us a home away from home during our many trips to M.D. Anderson Medical Center, and to Norm Wright for his valuable insights and for helping Gary with the Epilogue.

Thanks to our prayer warriors and to those who encouraged us through calling Carrie's prayer pager and through posting messages of encouragement on Carrie's Web site.

Thanks to the many couples who came to us for counsel and trusted us with the stories of their marriages, and the many couples who came to our seminars and workshops and encouraged us with their valuable feedback.

Thanks to our Lord Jesus Christ for His goodness, grace, mercy, patience, and for over twenty-five years of an intimate, passionate, enjoyable marriage relationship and for allowing us to experience the difference a Christ-centered marriage makes.

ABOUT THE AUTHORS

GARY J. OLIVER, ThM, PhD, a clinical psychologist with more than thirty years' experience in premarital, marital, and family counseling, is Executive Director of The Center for Relationship Enrichment and Professor of Psychology and Practical Theology at John Brown University, on the faculty of Denver Seminary, on the executive board and national speaking team of the American Association of Christian Counselors, and author or coauthor of more than fifteen books, including *Raising Sons and Loving It!* with his wife, Carrie, and *A Woman's Forbidden Emotion.* Gary lives in Siloam Springs, Arkansas.

CARRIE OLIVER, MA, was a wife, mom, teacher, university professor, and licensed professional counselor helping people develop healthy ways to deal with their emotions and relationships. Carrie spoke nationally and internationally, coauthored over 100 magazine articles and two other books, *Raising Sons and Loving It!* and *Grown-Up Girlfriends.* Gary and Carrie raised three sons together. Carrie passed away in July 2007 after a valiant battle with pancreatic cancer.

The Center *for* Relationship Enrichment

with Dr. Gary J. Oliver &
Dr. Greg Smalley

The Center for Relationship Enrichment (CRE) on the campus of John Brown University exists to cultivate healthy, Christ-centered relationships by educating, enriching, and equipping students, individuals, couples, families, churches and organizations through the transforming power of biblically-based consulting, education and enrichment at a local, regional, national and international level.

How do we know if we are being conformed to the image of Christ? Is the answer church involvement, learning Bible doctrine, or abstaining from sin? These are important but Christ is very clear about how we know if lives are being transformed in John 13:34-35: *"As I have loved you, so you must love one another. By this all men will know that you are my disciples, if you love one another."* As we become more Christ-like, the most powerful evidence is our ability to love others as Christ loves us.

UNIQUE CRE PROGRAMS

1. Church Relationships Assessment (CRA). The CRA is an assessment given to all adult attendees, both married and single, during a given Sunday morning church service. It provides a "fingerprint" of the congregation, where people are relationally, emotionally and spiritually, if they are growing and where they are growing. The CRA measures areas such as emotional intelligence, conflict management, communication, forgiveness, spirituality, marital and parenting satisfaction, and interest in growth opportunities. The CRA gives attendees an opportunity to identify and reflect on some of the most important areas in their lives and help them better understand what difference Christ is making in their lives and relationships. The comprehensive report gives leaders a more accurate understanding of your congregation's specific relational and spiritual strengths and needs, and how you can more effectively serve them and your church in strengthening individuals, marriages and families in the community.

2. LeaderCARE. LeaderCARE reaches out to church, ministry and business leaders and focuses on the unique struggles leaders face in maintaining a strong faith walk, healthy relationships, and effective leadership in the ministries or in the marketplace to which God has called them. CRE offers marriage intensives, multi-couple retreats, enrichment programs, training in emotional intelligence and consulting services.

3. Special Speaking Team. CRE's speaking team, including Dr. Gary Oliver and Dr. Greg and Erin Smalley, is well equipped to provide you with the necessary tools for enriching marriage and family relationships, train leadership teams and equip ministry leaders. We would enjoy the opportunity to discuss your specific needs and customize a speaking event that will have maximum impact for you.

For more information on these programs, or to inquire about speaking engagements, visit www.liferelationships.com or call 479-524-7105.